RADIOACTIVE HEAVEN AND EARTH

THE HEALTH AND ENVIRONMENTAL EFFECTS OF NUCLEAR WEAPONS TESTING IN, ON, AND ABOVE THE EARTH

RADIOACTIVE HEAVEN AND EARTH

The Health and Environmental Effects
of Nuclear Weapons Testing In, On,
and Above the Earth

A report of the IPPNW International Commission
To Investigate the Health and Environmental
Effects of Nuclear Weapons Production and the
Institute for Energy and Environmental Research

Commission Director
Anthony Robbins, M.D.
International Physicians for the Prevention
of Nuclear War

President of IEER and Technical
Consultant to Commission
Arjun Makhijani, Ph.D.
Institute for Energy and Environmental Research

Commission Coordinator
Katherine Yih, Ph.D.
International Physicians for the
Prevention of Nuclear War

THE APEX PRESS
New York

ZED BOOKS
London

The Apex Press is an imprint of the Council on International and Public Affairs, 777 United Nations Plaza,
New York, New York 10017 (212/953-6920).
Published in the United Kingdom by Zed Books Ltd.,
57 Caledonian Road, London N1 9BU.

British Library Cataloguing in Publication Data

International Physicians for the Prevention of Nuclear War.
International Commission
Radioactive heaven and earth : the health and environmental
effects of nuclear weapons testing in, on and above the earth :
a report of the IPPNW International Commission.
1. Public health. Effects of nuclear radiation
I. Title
363.1799

ISBN 1-85649-020-3
ISBN 1-85649-021-1 pbk

Library of Congress Cataloging-in-Publication Data

Radioactive heaven and earth : the health and environmental effects
of nuclear weapons testing in, on, and above the earth / International Physicians for the Prevention of Nuclear War, Inc., Institute for
Energy and Environmental Research.
        p.   cm.
    ISBN 0-945257-34-1
    1. Nuclear weapons--Testing--Health aspects. 2. Nuclear
weapons--Testing--Environmental aspects. I. International
Physicians for the Prevention of Nuclear War. II. Institute for
Energy and Environmental Research (Takoma Park, Md.)
RA569.R28 1991
363.17'992--dc20   90-25747
                                                            CIP

CONTENTS

PREFACE

In December 1988 the International Physicians for the Prevention of Nuclear War (IPPNW) created the Commission to study the health and environmental effects of nuclear weapons production. News accounts in the United States had revealed a nuclear weapons production complex replete with health, safety, and environmental problems. IPPNW reasoned that similar problems were likely to exist in all nuclear weapons producing countries and set out to get an overview of the size and scope of the problems.

The objective of the Commission has been to describe the health and environmental effects of nuclear weapons production and testing in scientific yet accessible terms, in order to provide the public with some understanding of the price it is paying simply to *build* nuclear weapons. The Commission's work will be a success if it encourages local groups of physicians, scientists, and environmentalists to pursue information and accountability at each site that has contributed to the pollution caused by nuclear weapons production. If these groups are successful, governments will respond by supporting intensive and extensive scientific investigations of the damage caused by nuclear weapons production and what must be done to protect the public from future harm.

Many groups and individuals have pitched in to help the Commission. The Commission has organized national task forces in several countries to help gather information and present Commission findings to the medical, scientific, and environmental community. The Physicians for Social Responsibility, IPPNW's affiliate organization in the United States, put together a task force at the same time the Commission was created, and colleagues in the Soviet Union, France, Britain, India, and China have all taken steps to organize national groups.

The production of nuclear weapons—from mining of uranium to fabrication and testing of bombs and warheads—has taken place at hundreds of sites around the world and has left a lasting mark on the planet. Because the task of quantifying the effects of the various components of the process on people and environment was enormous, the Commission divided the problem into more manageable pieces for study.

This first report of the Commission focuses on the health and environmental effects of two kinds of nuclear weapons testing: atmospheric tests (conducted before 1981) and underground tests. It concentrates on the testing programs of the United States, the Soviet Union, the United Kingdom, France, and China, the five acknowledged nuclear powers.

The Commission chose to highlight nuclear weapons testing in its first report for several reasons. There are better data available on weapons testing than on almost any other aspect of nuclear weapons production. Testing is a discrete issue and is most closely linked, along with weapons design, to continuation of the arms race. Testing is needed to build new and "better" nuclear weapons. A halt in testing would probably signal an end to the arms race in nuclear weapons. The release of this report also occurs in the year of the Test Ban Treaty Amendment Conference, when international interest in nuclear weapons testing is high.

Our study of nuclear weapons testing makes three original and important contributions to the information generally available to the public: 1) It recalculates the number of cancer cases and deaths expected from global scattering of fallout, using the new coefficients of the 1990 BEIR (Biological Effects of Ionizing Radiation) report;[1] 2) it provides a country-by-country review of nuclear weapons testing programs, including the decisions of where to test and the secrecy surrounding weapons testing; 3) the report calculates inventories of radionuclides left underground by underground testing. It points out, for the first time, the discrepancy between official attitudes toward long-term highly

---

1. National Research Council 1990.

radioactive wastes of military origin and those of civilian origin—only civilian waste repositories are subjected to careful scrutiny and public debate.

The report is intended for interested and concerned citizens. The sources of information are fully documented, and additional readings are provided for people who wish to explore the subject more deeply. We hope the book is an affirmation that, with persistence, citizens can penetrate the secrecy that has surrounded the development, production, and testing of nuclear weapons. This secrecy has extended far beyond military subjects, keeping the public ignorant about many health and environmental problems.

This report is only a start at comprehending the health and environmental consequences of nuclear weapons production. A subsequent report of the Commission will explore the issue of storage of high-level liquid radioactive waste in tanks, which presents a great hazard to health and environmental quality. In the end, the Commission plans to produce a comprehensive report covering all aspects of nuclear weapons production, where they occur in the world, and their effects on health and environment.

From a physician's point of view, the findings of the Commission are very disturbing. Nuclear weapons have been justified as a deterrent. They will never again be used, it is said. But as our investigations have considered health and environmental effects, as secrecy has been pierced here and there, the weapons production programs themselves are seen in a new light. There is evidence that conscious decisions were made to accept harm to people and to the environment in the pursuit of larger and more deadly nuclear arsenals. The need for military secrecy was inappropriately used to conceal information vital to protecting the public health. The report does not emphasize these observations about the morality of what was done. Rather, it tries to present the evidence. But for those who study the issue or read between the lines, this readiness to harm is omnipresent.

Greatest thanks for this report are due to Arjun Makhijani of the Institute for Energy and Environmental Research (IEER), who worked endlessly, setting and meeting incredible goals. He wrote or pieced together the bulk of this report. Victor Khokhryakov, Alex Shlyakhter, the Soviet Committee of Physicians for the Prevention of Nuclear War, and Masa Takubo translated sections of Soviet documents. Ted Taylor provided helpful information about nuclear weapons design. And we relied on a long list of distinguished reviewers to make suggestions, pick apart the document, and find mistakes before it reached the reader.

The IEER staff—Margaret Hawley, Scott Saleska, and Suzanne Aaron—were invaluable. Those at the IPPNW office who deserve special thanks and recognition are Katherine Yih for coordination and editing, Peter Zheutlin for editing, David Scott for coordination in the early stages of the project, Polly Parks for maps and cover design, Lynn Martin for photo research and copy editing, William Monning for mediation and team-building, and Norman Stein for his role in fundraising.

Anthony Robbins, M.D.
Director

ACKNOWLEDGEMENTS

This report was prepared under the direction of Anthony Robbins. A number of people wrote various sections or otherwise contributed to the work in major ways. They are, in alphabetical order:

John Andrews
Alexandra Brooks
Robin Briant
Bernd Franke
Graham Gulbransen
Charles Kerr
Arjun Makhijani
Anthony Robbins
Rob Robotham
Tilman Ruff
Stephan Schug
David Scott
Katherine Yih
Peter Zheutlin

The following organizations are gratefully acknowledged for their financial support of this project:

W. Alton Jones Foundation
John D. and Catherine T. MacArthur Foundation
Ruth Mott Fund
HKH Foundation
Svenska Läkare Mot Kärnvapen
(Swedish Physicians Against Nuclear Weapons)

Chapter 1

ASSESSING THE LEGACY OF NUCLEAR TESTING

Nuclear weapons testing plays a central role in the design of nuclear weapons. To date, six countries have conducted approximately 1,900 nuclear tests. Of these, about 518 have been in the atmosphere, under water, or in space. In 1963, the Treaty Banning Nuclear Weapon Tests in the Atmosphere, in Outer Space and Under Water, also called the Limited Test Ban Treaty or the Partial Test Ban Treaty, was signed by over 100 countries. The United States, Soviet Union, and United Kingdom, all signatories to the treaty, then moved their tests underground. France and China continued atmospheric tests after 1963—France until 1974 and China until 1980.

Approximately 1,400 tests have been conducted underground in scores of places around the globe. While these generally have much less dangerous immediate effects than atmospheric tests, they nevertheless leave long-lived radionuclides underground, some with half-lives of tens of thousands of years, which sooner or later may make their way into the biosphere.

Obtaining complete and accurate data on health and environmental effects of nuclear weapons testing is difficult. In large part this is because countries that have tested nuclear weapons gave the principal responsibility of assessing the health and environmental effects of the testing to the very agencies that make and test the weapons. These agencies have therefore found themselves with essentially contradictory missions. On the one hand, the reality of widespread fallout far from the explosions required people to be carefully informed about the nature of fallout, the dangers of radiation, and the possibility of intense radiation from rainouts. It required openness and full information and free discussion. But, the horrible effects of nuclear weapons and the difficulty of dealing with the unseen hazard of radiation often led these agencies to irresponsibility. The overwhelming desire for secrecy and the perceived need to build up nuclear arsenals often prevailed. The very first public announcement of nuclear weapons was, after all, the destruction of Hiroshima in one blinding flash.

Except for at very high doses, radiation damage is not immediately apparent. Most of the damage occurs over years, decades, and even centuries, after which causal connections are difficult to establish. The secrecy around nuclear weapons production, preventing public knowledge of exposures, has made it even harder for people to associate recent effects with exposures of decades ago. Considerable damage is done to health and the environment before the public becomes aware.

During the period of atmospheric testing in the United States, radiation protection limits on doses to participants in nuclear weapons programs were set higher than radiation protection guidelines for civilians, and even these high limits were regularly exceeded. For example, in the early days of U.S. nuclear weapons testing, the official limit was 3.9 rads per year for the public downwind of atmospheric tests, but in practice, as we shall see, action tended not to be taken until doses reached or exceeded the level at which immediate radiation symptoms became manifest. That level is about 100 rads, about 25 times the official dose limit.

The pattern of secrecy makes the task of assessing the effects of nuclear weapons testing on this and future generations a particularly difficult one. Yet despite the handicaps, some information has become public. In the United States public concern began early on, taking on special intensity after heavy fallout from the 1954 U.S. thermonuclear test in the Marshall Islands irradiated the crew of a Japanese fishing boat, the *Lucky Dragon* and seriously contaminated the atoll of Rongelap. Lawsuits and protests by victims of testing have also played a big role in breaking the veil of secrecy. In the case of Britain, it was a commission of inquiry in Australia, where British tests were conducted, that yielded the most significant information and analysis.

The shroud of secrecy is beginning to dissolve in the Soviet Union as well. The Chernobyl accident extended *glasnost* to the nuclear arena, and information is now becoming available, although sometimes confusing or contradictory.

Of the five major nuclear weapons states, only France and China have not yet made public information about fallout, hot spots, or irradiation from their atmospheric nuclear weapons testing programs. Information about nuclear testing and its effects is still firmly in the hands of the military and nuclear establishments of these countries.

* * *

It is useful to separate all nuclear weapons tests into two categories: 1) atmospheric, surface, space, and underwater tests, which for the purposes of this report we call collectively "atmospheric" tests, and 2) underground tests. Both categories of tests spread radiation in the environment and expose people, although via different routes. Venting of radioactivity to the atmosphere from underground tests creates some overlap between the two categories.

In this introductory chapter, the basic technical background important for understanding the production of radioactivity by nuclear explosions and health effects is presented. (The glossary provided at the back of the report may also be of help in interpreting the more technical sections of this study.) We then discuss some of the problems in assessing the effects of atmospheric and underground testing. In the following chapter, we discuss our methodology.

Technical Background

Nuclear Explosions and Their Results

Nuclear explosions result from the sudden conversion of a small portion of the mass of nuclei of atoms into energy. The amount of energy released is given by Einstein's famous formula $E = mc^2$. There are two different kinds of nuclear processes which can result in such a sudden release of energy: (1) fission of heavy nuclei, and (2) fusion of light nuclei.

Nuclear weapons can be made using only fission as the basis for nuclear energy release, or with some combination of fission and fusion components. Nuclear fission is the process by which the nucleus of an atom is split apart when it is bombarded by some form of energy—usually a neutron. A chain reaction occurs when each fission of an atom results in at least one neutron that produces another fission reaction (on the average). When a sufficiently large mass of such a material, known as fissile material, is assembled in a suitable shape and density, it can be made to "go critical"—that is, sustain a nuclear chain reaction without further stimulation from external events. If a fissile material is compressed to a high enough density, it can be made to go supercritical where a sufficient number of fission events happen in a short enough time for the mass to explode, releasing a huge amount of energy.

There are two principal fissile materials: uranium-235 and plutonium-239. Uranium-235 occurs in nature in association with uranium-238 (in a ratio of 0.7 percent uranium-235 to 99.3 percent uranium-238). It must be enriched to about 90 percent uranium-235 to make compact nuclear weapons. Plutonium-239 is almost entirely man-made and is made from uranium-238 in nuclear reactors. Both uranium-235 and plutonium-239 emit alpha radiation, but plutonium-239 is more radioactive, emitting 30,000 times more alpha radiation than uranium-235 per unit of mass. (The various kinds of radiation are described below.) Uranium-238 can also be fissioned by bombarding it with neutrons, but it cannot sustain a chain reaction by itself. It is used as a supplementary material to increase the explosive yield of some nuclear weapons. The chain reaction in a fission weapon can be triggered by a conventional explosive charge.

Each fission of a uranium or plutonium-239 atom produces two or three fission fragments of lighter elements, each known as a fission product. Most of these fission fragments are radioactive. They decay into other elements, emitting beta and gamma radiation, until they reach a form that is non-radioactive (or stable).

Most radioactive fission products have very short half-lives of a few minutes or less. (Half-life is a term used to describe the amount of time that it takes for an element to release half of its radioactivity, decaying to another element or isotope.) However, some fission products have half-lives extending into hours, days, years, decades, or more. Among the more prevalent fission products with relatively short half-lives are some of the noble gases like xenon-133 (half-life: 5.25 days) and xenon-135 (half-life: 9.1 hours), as well as iodine-131 (half-life: 8 days). Among the more prevalent fission products with relatively long half-lives are strontium-90 (half-life: 28.8 years) and cesium-137 (half-life: 30.2 years).

Nuclear weapons that release a large portion of their energy in fusion reactions are called thermonuclear weapons or, more popularly, hydrogen (H) bombs. The dominant fusion reactions are between isotopes of hydrogen—deuterium and tritium. The fusion reaction cannot be triggered by a conventional charge alone. To get hydrogen isotopes to fuse in sufficient quantities rapidly enough to produce an explosion requires very high temperatures, like those in the interior of the sun. Therefore, thermonuclear weapons use a fission component with plutonium-239 or uranium-235 to trigger the fusion reaction. The main radioactive contaminants from thermonuclear weapons come from the fission triggers and any uranium-238, uranium-235, or plutonium-239 close enough to the fusion portion of the weapon to be split by neutrons from the fusion reaction. In the case of a 1-megaton H-bomb, the fission trigger contributes only about 3 percent of the radioactive contamination; the rest comes from the uranium-238 tamper.

A third type of weapon is called a boosted fission weapon. Although it derives its energy principally from fission, it uses a small amount of tritium and deuterium to boost the number of neutrons and therefore the amount of fission. Boosted fission explosives are widely used as triggers for thermonuclear weapons.

Total Fission Product Activity and Decay[1]

The mix of fission products that nuclear weapons release depends on the design of the weapon, not on the location of the testing. The principal difference between atmospheric and underground tests, when there is no venting, is that the short-lived radionuclides do not contribute to adverse health impacts in the case of underground testing. Of course, if there is substantial venting, then this distinction between underground and atmospheric testing disappears.

How does one estimate the amount of radioactive material produced by nuclear weapons tests? A 1-kiloton explosion (explosive force equal to 1,000 tons of TNT) will typically produce 41 billion curies of radioactive fission products one minute after detonation and this will be reduced to 10 million curies in 12 hours, as the short-lived radionuclides decay.[2] The equation that defines the decay of fission

---

1. For more details on the material in this and the next section, see Glasstone and Dolan 1977, Chapters 8 and 9.
2. U.S. Congress, Office of Technology Assessment 1989, p. 60.

products is remarkably simple:

$$R(t) = R_o \cdot t^{-1.2}$$
where
R(t) is the radioactivity in curies at time t in hours, and
R_o is the radioactivity one hour after the explosion.

The quantities R can also be expressed in other units of radioactivity such as rads per hour.

The above equation estimates the radioactivity resulting from fission products that constitute the overwhelming majority of the radioactivity in the hours, days, and weeks following a nuclear explosion.

Induced Radioactivity

The most important source of radionuclides other than fission products and alpha emitters is induced radioactivity. Induced radioactive materials result from the bombardment of non-radioactive materials by some of the neutrons generated during the fission and fusion reactions. Radioactivity is induced in non-radioactive materials used in nuclear weapons as well as those in the surrounding environment. Thus, unlike the composition of fission products, the composition of induced radioactive materials depends on the test location.

The most important radionuclide resulting from atmospheric testing is carbon-14, with a half-life of 5,730 years. Carbon-14 results from a nuclear reaction involving the capture of a neutron by nitrogen and the emission of a proton:

nitrogen-14 + neutron → carbon-14 + proton

This reaction has created a large amount of induced carbon-14 radioactivity in the atmosphere due to the abundance of nitrogen. (Carbon-14 is a beta emitter.) Some carbon-14 is also created by underground testing, though it is far less important than in the case of atmospheric testing.

Another important radionuclide created by neutron capture is sodium-24. This reaction is important in the case of ocean testing of nuclear weapons. Sodium-23, the natural isotope of sodium in sea salt, is converted to radioactive sodium-24 by the absorption of a neutron.

sodium-23 + neutron → sodium-24

Sodium-24, with a half-life of 15 hours, emits highly energetic beta radiation (4 mega-electron volts [4 MeV]) which can penetrate the skin and is associated with lymphatic system cancer. Some tests may have caused high exposures to sodium-24. For example, due to lax radiological safety (called in one memo of Operation Crossroads "a hairy-chested . . . disdain for the unseen hazard" on the part of naval officers), some armed forces personnel were allowed to swim in Bikini lagoon soon after the underwater test Baker, exposing them not only to fission products and plutonium-239 but also to sodium-24.[3]

The bombardment of nitrogen by fast neutrons also results in the creation of tritium (which is a radioactive isotope of hydrogen) and nonradioactive carbon-12:

$$\text{nitrogen-14} + \text{neutron} \quad \rightarrow \quad \text{carbon-12} + \text{tritium}$$

Radiation Exposure Due to Testing

There are four types of radiation that result from nuclear explosions: (1) gamma radiation, which is electromagnetic energy of high frequency; (2) beta radiation, which consists of energetic electrons; (3) alpha radiation, which consists of helium ions produced by the radioactive disintegration of heavy nuclei like plutonium-239; and (4) neutrons, which are produced by the nuclear reactions that take place during the explosion. Of these, the first three are produced by the radioactive decay of fission products, of heavy elements like plutonium-239, and of materials with induced radioactivity. Neutrons decay rapidly into a proton and an electron. They directly affect living beings only in the immediate vicinity of the explosions. Their indirect effect via induced radioactivity is, however, very important, especially in the production of carbon-14.

Gamma radiation is highly penetrating and will pass through paper or wood, but it is stopped by lead or thick concrete. It is essentially X-rays of high frequency. Beta radiation is not very penetrating. External exposure to beta radiation affects the skin and, in the case of very energetic beta radiation, tissues a few millimeters below the skin surface are also affected. Alpha radiation is even less penetrating. Beta and alpha emitters produce most of their damage if they are incorporated into the body, damaging the organs and cells in the immediate vicinity of where

---

3. Makhijani and Albright 1983.

they are lodged.

The quantity of fallout in the immediate vicinity of an explosion and in the downwind areas is critically dependent on the type of test. When weapons are exploded at or just above the surface of land, large amounts of soil and other debris are carried upwards in the mushroom cloud. This dust carries radioactive particles with it, and this radioactivity comes back down as fallout when the dust settles. In high-altitude explosions, there is no entrainment of dust and fallout consists of particles that disperse, settling out of the atmosphere gradually because of their higher density. The deposition of radioactivity is enhanced in areas where there is heavy rain at the time the radioactive cloud is passing overhead.

Underwater tests, especially shallow underwater tests and tests at or near the surface of the water, produce large quantities of radioactive spray. This spray results in the contamination of any structures or land areas nearby and contamination of the water body in which the test is carried out. Tests in shallow water also result in the scouring up of sand from the bottom that is then carried along with the spray and deposited on land or ships nearby. Another effect of tests under, on, or above the ocean is to produce induced radioactivity in the form of sodium-24.

The most important short-lived radionuclide in terms of dose to a particular organ is iodine-131, with a half-life of eight days. Iodine-131 is inhaled directly from the air. It is also concentrated in milk when cattle graze on grass where it has been deposited in fallout. When this contaminated milk is consumed, the iodine enters the bloodstream and subsequently concentrates in the thyroid. Iodine-131 decays by emitting beta radiation. In the process, it also emits gamma radiation.

Radioisotopes of intermediate half-life that are important in delivering doses from fallout are zirconium-95 (half-life: 64 days); cerium-144 (half-life: 284 days); and ruthenium-106 (half-life: 367 days). The most important long-lived fission products are cesium-137 and strontium-90. All of these radionuclides deliver doses when they are inhaled from air containing them, from resuspended dust, and from ingestion after they become incorporated into the food chain. Most of them also deliver external gamma radiation doses.

Severe damage to people in downwind areas and to test site personnel can occur due to deposition of large quantities of radioactive materials on their bodies. Fallout in the vicinity of test sites contains large quantities of short-lived radionuclides. Such deposition typically results in high gamma doses to the whole body, as well as high doses to the skin from beta radiation.

Carbon-14 is the longest lived of the major radioactive products of nuclear explosions. Carbon-14 is produced when atmospheric nitrogen absorbs a neutron. Thus, when carbon-14 is created, it is in gaseous form due to the very nature of the process of its formation from gaseous nitrogen. This carbon soon becomes converted to carbon dioxide and is taken up by plants and incorporated into organic material and the food chain.

Plutonium-239 is a highly toxic emitter of alpha radiation. Thus, despite the relatively small amounts of plutonium-239 deposited in terms of total radioactivity, it is still a source of great concern. This is especially so in many of the areas near atmospheric test locations and immediately downwind.

How radiation doses are delivered to living beings by incorporation of radioactive materials is affected by the biological half-life of these materials. Once a radioactive material is consumed or inhaled and becomes part of the body, it is slowly expelled along with other materials. The amount of time during which half of the material is expelled from the body is known as the biological half-life. Thus, there are two modes by which a radioactive material is eliminated from the body: one is physical decay of the material itself; and the other is its rate of elimination from the body. These rates are additive.[4]

Measurement Problems Related to Atmospheric Testing

Several problems make it very difficult to describe accurately the effects, both health and environmental, of atmospheric nuclear weapons tests. Secrecy precludes an adequate data base everywhere and causes almost total obscurity in some countries, namely France and China, which have released practically no information on fallout in communities downwind from their tests.

In countries where information has been made public, it is often inadequate to provide a complete picture of human exposure. Some data were never collected. Gamma radiation was monitored more extensively than beta and alpha radiation. Measurements of internal radiation, such as whole body counting, are usually too scanty to provide an ade-

---

4. The net half-life, T_n, is given by the expression $1/T_n = 1/T_r + 1/T_b$, where T_r is physical half-life due to radioactive decay and T_b is the biological half-life.

quate picture of exposure.

The geographic distribution of fallout was also poorly described by monitoring networks. Monitoring was usually best near the test explosions, but monitoring points became sparse at greater distances from test sites. The limited number of monitoring points makes it impossible to describe the localized variations in exposure that depended on weather.

These flaws in measurement have their greatest effect on studies that depend on accurate information about the exposure of people and precision in individual or small group dose estimates. For example, if a few highly exposed individuals are overlooked and omitted from the exposed population, the population dose is underestimated. Results may then understate the true exposure of the population or discover health effects that seem inexplicably high using the underestimated dose. Failure to discover the heavily irradiated areas and highly exposed individuals has often supported decisions not to proceed with health studies or follow the population medically.

Lack of good exposure measurements has also encouraged the use of simplified and weaker epidemiologic methods. For example, when comparing a population involved in a nuclear weapons test with a population not involved, the results may depend on how the involved population is chosen. If it is too inclusive, the study design will dilute a truly exposed group with individuals defined as involved but who are not truly exposed. Then the difference between the exposed and unexposed groups will appear less than it is.

Doses to Test Personnel and Downwinders

How can doses received shortly after atmospheric tests be estimated? In the United States, three general assumptions were made, which affected official estimates of radiation dose and associated health risks:

1. that beta and gamma radiation levels were proportional to each other;
2. that internal doses were generally insignificant compared to gamma doses;
3. that deposition of radioactivity on the ground was an adequate indicator of radioactivity in the air and therefore an adequate predictor of internal doses.

There is now substantial evidence that all three assumptions were misleading and often just plain wrong. Moreover, there is also evidence, at least in the United States, where the relevant documents are public, that officials responsible for radiological safety knew these assumptions were not appropriately conservative from the public health point of view and, in fact, were incorrect.

Official calculations of doses tended to assume that external gamma radiation was the principal source of radiation for both test personnel and downwind communities, leading to a failure to measure, or a grave underestimation of, the quantities and hazards of beta radiation and internal (alpha, beta, and gamma) radiation. The assumption that beta radiation was proportional to gamma radiation was found to be mistaken fairly early on; this discovery did not, however, alter official measurement practices.

Karl Morgan, who headed the Health Physics department at the U.S. government's Oak Ridge National Laboratory and was in charge of measuring radiation levels after several of the tests, wrote in 1951:

> After eight years of experience dealing directly with problems of survey work and after making thousands of field surveys myself and many calculations of one sort or another, I have been convinced that there are certain practical problems of survey monitoring that are not necessarily obvious.... [D]uring the period following the underwater test at Bikini [in July 1946] . . . those in charge of monitoring were instructing personnel that the beta hazard would be directly proportional to the gamma hazard; that it would not be necessary to make beta ray evaluation. . . .
>
> Fortunately, I had taken with me about 20 instruments from our laboratory that were well suited to the measurement of beta to gamma ratio. . . . Most places aboard ship the beta to gamma ratio ranged from three to 10. Some places it ran as high as 1,000. Many places the ratio was from 50 to 100. Wherever we found tar, paint, rust, rosin, wood, fabric, plankton, barnacles, etc. there was a selective absorption of the beta products as against the gamma emitting radioisotopes.[5]

Karl Morgan had filed an official report on his radiation measurements at Operation Crossroads at Bikini in 1946. Yet many years later, the official position still was that the beta-to-gamma radiation ratio could be considered a constant, and that it was not necessary to make measurements of beta radiation levels.

---

5. Karl Morgan in letter to Giacchino Failla, January 24, 1951, cited in Allen 1984, p. 226.

Bruce S. Jenkins, the Federal judge who presided over a lawsuit filed against the U.S. government by several people who lived downwind of the Nevada Test Site, summarized the situation regarding gamma and beta monitoring as follows:

> Monitoring instruments were often calibrated to the "hard" high-energy gamma rays...and used to take quick readings of external gamma exposure rates. Little attention was directed to careful monitoring of lower energy gamma rays, or to measurement of beta radiation or determination of beta/gamma ratios. On occasion, off-site monitors were specifically instructed to work with the metal beta shields on their instruments completely closed....Monitoring of beta activities was largely left to the air sampling activities of aerial monitoring or mechanical air-sampling stations.[6]

Similarly, the deposition of alpha emitters, specifically plutonium-239, was not well measured. At Operation Crossroads, the first nuclear weapons test series after the Second World War, there were no field instruments that could measure alpha radiation adequately. As Colonel Stafford Warren, Chief of Radiological Safety at the test series, noted:

> Every contaminated place as evidenced by the gamma or beta radiation on any surface of any vessel may in fact be the residence of many lethal doses of this alpha emitter [plutonium-239]. This alpha emitter is the most poisonous chemical known. It can only be measured with very precise equipment which is not available and cannot be made available.[7]

During the whole of the atmospheric testing program, there was no routine monitoring of plutonium-239.[8]

The failure to measure plutonium-239, beta emitters, and in many cases, "soft" gamma radiation meant that the most important sources of internal radiation from inhalation and ingestion, where even small burdens of radioactive materials could result in large local doses to specific parts of the body, were not made. Reviewing this situation in 1981, Bernard Schleien of the U.S. Food and Drug Administration wrote:

> Internal exposure from inhalation and ingestion, and its contribution to the radiation exposure of the off-site population around the NTS [Nevada Test Site] has not been determined.[9]

---

6. Allen 1984, pp. 254-255.
7. Warren 1946.
8. Allen 1984.
9. Schleien 1981, p. 243.

TROOPS AT OPERATION BUSTER, NEVADA TEST SITE, USA, NOVEMBER 1, 1951.
Photo: Defense Nuclear Agency

Official calculations have tended to assume that the deposition of radioactivity on the ground was an adequate indicator of radioactivity in the air and therefore an adequate predictor of internal doses. This assumption has not been borne out by experience.

Some field measurements were taken long after the atmospheric test series were complete. However, due to washing off by rain and snow, as well as scattering by winds, measurements made after long periods may find more uniform distribution than the original patterns of deposition. If this is so, dose estimates based on such measurements would usually tend to underestimate, perhaps seriously in some cases, the doses received in areas where deposition may have been initially high.

Furthermore, patterns of deposition do not necessarily correlate with airborne radioactivity. Deposition not only depends on how much radioactivity there is in the air, but on the specific weather conditions and particle sizes. This problem was discovered in the very first test series in Nevada in 1951, code-named Ranger:

> If a man happened to be actually in the path of the low-flying dust-cloud, he could measure significant amounts of radioactivity while airborne particles, very small in size, were actually around him. When the dust cloud had passed, there seemed to be *little or nothing deposited on the ground and no residual activity of any significance.*[10]

People who were outdoors, and particularly those who were breathing heavily when highly radioactive clouds were present, may have received heavy doses, both internally by inhalation and externally from gamma radiation from short-lived fission products. These doses would not have been registered by passive monitoring equipment dependent on precipitation of radioactive particles to detect the dose. This discrepancy between deposited radioactivity and actual doses received would be accentuated by the fact that it is the smaller particles that would be breathed in but not deposited in corresponding quantities. Additionally, these particles deliver larger inhalation doses because they pass farther down the bronchial tree and are more likely to be trapped and deposited in the lungs.

Even data on external gamma radiation, considered most important in the official calculations, are problematic. For instance, sometimes

---

10. Allen 1984, p. 452, footnote 133, emphasis added.

personnel who participated in the tests did not wear film badges to measure gamma radiation doses. During the tests at Bikini in 1946, the Medico-Legal Board, a government group which reviewed health effects of tests, noted that it was "most likely that a number of persons not carrying film badges were likewise overexposed."[11] In the United States, much of the badge data that did exist has been lost or destroyed. Badge data that remain are questionable because readings were not reproducible, often due to badge quality. According to the U.S. General Accounting Office (GAO) investigation of the test series code-named Redwing:

> ... problems were identified with some of the film badges used, particularly at Operations Tumbler-Snapper and Redwing. For instance, about 10 years after the film badge's use at Tumbler-Snapper, the manufacturer reported that the badge's two film components could not effectively measure radiation between 4 to 9 rem.

> In addition GAO found errors in about 26 percent and 13 percent of the records used to tabulate the readings from all film badges worn by personnel at operations Redwing and Dominic I, respectively.[12]

To estimate exposures in the absence of good data, it has been necessary to resort to "dose reconstruction," which relies on such data as do exist and on other information regarding the nature of the activities of specific personnel during specific tests. Such dose reconstruction is useful and feasible in some cases but cannot be applied credibly to the vast majority of cases where critical data are simply non-existent.

Hot Spots

About half the fallout from atmospheric testing returned to earth near the test sites and in the downwind areas within a few hundred kilometers of the test locations. The rest was deposited around the globe. The deposition of fallout over the globe was non-uniform. Some unknown portion of the radioactive material that did not return to earth near the test site also failed to stay suspended in the atmosphere long enough to become evenly dispersed. This portion was deposited in hot spots where rain and other weather conditions brought the fallout rapidly back to earth—unpredictably, since it was impossible to predict the

---

11. Medico-Legal Board of Operation Crossroads 1946.
12. U.S. General Accounting Office 1987.

weather accurately more than a few hours after any detonation. These hot spots account for only a very small portion of the one half of radiation that is called "global." Yet it may have been sufficient in regions of heavy rainout to expose people over a few days to doses equivalent to a year or more of the fully dispersed fallout.

A.R. Tamplin—then at the Lawrence Livermore National Laboratory, where nuclear weapons were and are designed—made the following observations in 1966 about hot spots from U.S. testing:

> ... "hot spots" from tropospheric clouds have occurred either by dry deposition of particles or by rainout. Those developed by dry deposition are often associated with a prolonged residence time of the radioactive particles in the area. This is a result of the interplay between meteorological and topographical factors. Rainout "hot spots," of course, occur when a [fallout] cloud intersects a rain storm. In each case the magnitude of the hot spot is dependent upon the concentration of the radioactive material in the cloud coupled with the dry deposition rate or the fraction removed by rainfall.[13]

Hot spots have been detected by fallout monitoring networks set up at various locations. They have occurred hundreds or even thousands of kilometers away from the test locations. For instance, the intense hot spot created over Albany, New York in 1953, about 4,000 kilometers from the Nevada Test Site, was detected by a station that was part of the U.S. monitoring network (see Chapter 4). However, in most of the world the monitoring network that uses gummed film detectors to which particles stick was much thinner than in the United States. Thus, it is probable that large numbers of hot spots with initial radioactivity levels thousands or millions of times greater than average levels have occurred throughout the globe as a result of atmospheric nuclear weapons testing. The location of these hot spots, and the victims who live in some of them, will in most cases remain unknown. This was indeed the official conclusion from the analysis of the intense and unexpected Albany fallout:

> Because of the many unknowns involved, initial concentration, particle-sized [sic] distribution, terminal velocities, scavenging efficiency, eddy diffusion, wind shear, etc., it is impossible to make valid quantitative estimates of the maximum fallout or rainout likely to occur from continental tests....[I]n view of the Albany case, no conclusions were reached concerning maximum possible rainout and it

---

13. Tamplin 1966, p. 7.

is very likely that certain combinations of circumstances can bring about surface depositions many times larger than have been heretofore observed from continental tests.[14]

Because of testing locations, the vast area of the oceans, and the location of population and monitoring stations, most undetected hot spots are likely to have occurred over rural areas, uninhabited areas, or over the oceans. Of these locations, the most important for health considerations would be the ones in rural areas, where people may have been subjected to high doses from short-lived radionuclides and where there might be pockets of intense long-lived radioactivity as well. The highly localized nature of hot spots and their remote location make it unlikely that they would be found without immense efforts and perhaps not even then.

There are probably a large number of undetected hot spots around the world, and people in hot spot locations may have received doses of radiation comparable to the immediate downwind communities and far above the average global dose. Hypothetical assessments of such doses are possible, and in Chapter 4 we use an official U.S. document to illustrate one such case.

Practical Problems in Estimating Radiation Dose

Each individual included in epidemiologic studies was differently exposed because of location, protection such as clothing, and activity. Epidemiologic studies evaluate health and disease in individuals and groups to whom the researcher has assigned a measured or estimated dose received. The practical problems in assigning a correct dose affect the value of the studies.

The experience at Operation Crossroads provides an illustration of variation in exposure. About 42,000 personnel, mainly from the U.S. armed forces, participated in Operation Crossroads at Bikini in 1946, but most likely only an unidentified few percent were exposed to high levels of radiation. This test series was slated to consist of three nuclear explosions, but the third was cancelled due to serious radioactive contamination of the fleet after the second test, Baker, which was a shallow underwater test.[15]

---

14. List 1954, p. 65.
15. For an account of radiological conditions during Operation Crossroads based on official documents, see Makhijani and Albright 1983.

Test Baker sent highly radioactive spray and radioactive waves over the "target" ships, which were anchored in the lagoon. These waves also washed over some of the beaches of Bikini. The personnel were on "non-target" ships some miles away. The non-target ships were moved into the contaminated lagoon at various times after the test. Stafford Warren (Chief Radiological Safety Officer for the testing agency) discovered unpredictable and uneven deposition of plutonium-239 contamination on target ships. Because there was no good way to measure alpha emitters in the field, there was no way to protect personnel in the areas of high plutonium-239 contamination as they went about their work. Areas within short distances of one another had contamination levels that differed by an order of magnitude or more. A pile of coral sand scoured from the bottom and deposited on one target ship gave a reading of 200 roentgens per day 20 days after the underwater test. (This was 2,000 times the allowable limit of exposure to personnel.) Some materials like wood decks and manila rope retained radioactive contaminants. Thus, the radioactivity was spread out very unevenly and unpredictably.

Furthermore, the dose received by personnel would have been highly contingent on their specific activities. Some of the personnel were put to scrubbing down highly contaminated ships, with highly variable levels of contamination. Others ate or slept on board contaminated ships. Others were stationed on beaches that had been contaminated by radioactive spray and waves. On one ship, Karl Morgan observed that meat was being washed with radioactive water, which probably led to different internal doses depending on how much and what part was eaten by whom.

As another example of the practical difficulty in assigning doses to individuals, a small portion of the personnel who participated in the Operation Redwing test series in the Marshall Islands in 1956 flew through the intensely radioactive mushroom clouds 15 minutes or so after the tests, in an experiment designed to study nuclear war fighting capabilities of aircraft crews. A small number of other personnel hosed down the highly contaminated aircraft, generally without protective gear. These two sub-groups were probably at considerably greater risk of exposure to high doses than the other participants—the first sub-group to high external gamma doses, the second to high inhalation doses. However, unless identified, they cannot be assigned appropriate doses when included in studies.

Similarly, one could expect to find groups of people among downwinders or at hot spots who were much more highly exposed than the average. For instance, the children who were outdoors during the heavy fallout from the 1953 U.S. test at Nevada that came to be known as "Dirty Harry" received far greater doses than those who were indoors.

In all these cases the problem is not one of determining the response of people to low doses of radiation, but rather of identifying the groups of people who had been highly exposed. Studies of such identified individuals are more likely to find effects of radiation from nuclear weapons testing in participants and downwind residents than studies in which the highly exposed people are not distinguished from the others. Yet the difficulty in assigning the correct exposure to individuals frequently led to reliance on simplified and inadequate epidemiologic studies, which often treated personnel who participated in tests as a homogeneous group and then compared them with a control group of non-participants.

A study of veterans of British testing in Australia provides an illustration.[16] The study considered about 22,000 test personnel and had a control group of 22,000. It showed a weak correlation between certain radiogenic cancers and participation in the nuclear tests. However, the study did not identify individuals with heavy exposure or determine what the rate of cancer was in the sub-population of heavily exposed participants. (See Chapter 7 for details of this study.) For instance, personnel who worked with equipment located near the test for experimental purposes may have received very high doses of radiation due to the induced radioactivity in such equipment. Professor James Falk of Wollongong University in Australia calculated that radiation readings from the radiators of trucks may have reached 200 rads per hour shortly after the tests due to induced radioactivity in copper. However, the short half-life of copper-64 (12.7 hours) precluded accurate estimates of exposure, as they would depend on the exact time at which a particular person was near or in such equipment.[17]

Dose and exposure measurement problems can affect the outcome of epidemiologic studies in either direction. If one fails to add higher local doses to the population dose total, the number of cancers observed, for example, will seem to have been caused by a lower dose. When highly exposed individuals are diluted in a large and less exposed population, the study may suggest that the total exposed population was

---

16. Darby et al. 1988b.
17. Prof. James Falk, University of Wollongong, Australia, personal communication, October 7, 1990.

little different from the control population. In either case, the problems of estimating exposure and identifying highly exposed individuals reduce the utility of epidemiologic studies as a way to understand the effects of radiation in general and on specific populations.

Measurement Problems Related to Underground Testing

There are two principal ways in which the radiation from underground testing may affect human health and the environment. The most immediate is the fallout from atmospheric releases of radioactivity that often occur with underground tests. The second arises from the long-lived radionuclides that are left underground.

Atmospheric Contamination After Underground Tests

Underground testing of nuclear weapons has resulted in releases of radioactive fission products to the atmosphere. Some releases were not anticipated and were therefore uncontrolled, while others were deliberate. Again using the United States as the best documented example, the U.S. Congressional Office of Technology Assessment has classified releases into four groups:[18]

1. Containment Failures: unintentional releases of radioactive material to the atmosphere due to the failure of the containment system. These are termed "venting" if they are prompt, massive releases, or "seeps" if they are slow, small releases that occur soon after the test.
2. Late-Time Seeps: small releases that occur days or weeks after a test when gases diffuse through pore spaces of the overlying rock and are drawn to the surface by decreases in atmospheric pressure.
3. Controlled Tunnel Purgings: intentional releases to allow either recovery of experimental data and equipment or the reuse of part of the tunnel system.
4. Operational Releases: small releases that occur during opera-

---

18. U.S. Congress, Office of Technology Assessment 1989.

tions such as collection of gas samples.

We will focus on the unintentional releases because these have caused the largest discharges of radioactivity to the atmosphere.

Underground Accumulations

To assess how and when radioactive materials will reach the human environment once they are deposited underground by a nuclear test is much more difficult than for atmospheric testing. The uncertainties we face in this task are similar to those of assessing the pathways by which nuclear wastes disposed of underground would reach the human environment. In other words, the methodological approach is essentially the same as that of assessing the effects of wastes placed in a repository.

Non-Radiological Effects of Underground Testing

There are a number of ways in which underground testing can affect environment and human health adversely. The non-radiological factors include negative economic and social impacts on communities. For instance, communities become economically dependent on a military activity that destroys the long-term integrity of the environment, leaving it to generations far into the future to deal with the mess left underground. Other aspects are region-specific. For instance, physical destruction of coral reefs due to construction and other testing-related activity can cause poisons to accumulate in fish in the Pacific atolls, where the United States, French, and British have conducted nuclear weapons testing, as we discuss in the respective chapters.

Chapter 2

METHODOLOGY

In this chapter we discuss our overall approach to assessing the effects of nuclear weapons testing, including an explanation of why we include tests with non-military objectives, how we estimate cancer deaths and the cancer risk from nuclear weapons tests, and what other considerations we use in assessing effects of atmospheric and underground testing.

General Approach

In estimating health and environmental effects of weapons testing, we:

1. Used existing data that are sound and not the subject of dispute. Such data include official information on the locations and numbers of tests; some data on yields and types of weapons, including estimates of the size of the fission component; data on the types of tests; some local air monitoring data; and estimates of the total radioactivity in fallout and its composition, with an approximate division between local and global fallout.

2. Made conservative estimates of global doses from atmospheric testing by assuming uniform fallout over large areas. More refined estimates would take into account hot spots, due to rainouts of radioactivity, for example.
3. Made order-of-magnitude estimates of an overall source term for the tests conducted by each testing country. This enables a calculation of the approximate levels of radionuclides and their rate of decay. We also discuss an approximate partitioning of this source term between "local" and "global." In that context, we present a qualitative discussion of hot spots far from test locations due to rainouts and dry deposition of radioactivity in the United States and Soviet Union.
4. Took into account the testimony of witnesses and victims regarding their own experiences, location at the time of the tests, and health and environmental phenomena. While such descriptions are generally not sufficient for dose calculations, they can help establish that certain types of health effects may be linked to nuclear weapons tests. Eyewitness reports may help identify and define high exposure groups.
5. Took into account uncertainties regarding doses and environmental effects due to lack of data or poor or uncertain data. For instance, field measurements of alpha emitters beyond and often within test areas are very meager. Similarly, studies of undersea and underground testing environments are either lacking or highly uncertain.
6. Considered downwind communities (whose inhabitants sometimes call themselves "downwinders") separately from test site workers and civilian and military participants in the tests, reflecting the separation that exists in the research that has been done. The effects on the two populations can be quite similar, however.

Counting Nuclear Tests Which Include Non-Military Objectives

We include in our analysis both tests with explicitly military objectives and those with supposedly civilian objectives, such as the Plowshare series in the United States, a similar series in the Soviet Union, and a single test in India. We did so because tests with civilian objectives (such as digging canals or stimulating natural gas production) can also yield information for the design and production of nuclear weapons.

As Carter and Moghissi noted in their article reviewing the first three decades of nuclear testing:

> The testing of nuclear devices is usually for the purposes of gaining knowledge of nuclear explosive phenomena and of effects of nuclear detonations. . . . [I]t is reasonable to assume that most tests may have multiple purposes.
>
> A major division of nuclear tests has been between those for peaceful purposes and military applications. This may be a technical distinction. It would be prudent to assume that any announced test for peaceful purposes could have military overtones.[1]

We have therefore deemed it appropriate to include all tests as having at least an implicit military aspect, irrespective of the announced objective.

Estimates of Adverse Health Effects

There are a number of adverse health consequences of radiation. High levels of radiation (a few hundred rads) delivered over short periods result in severe injury and often death within hours or days. Lower levels of radiation have delayed effects—the best known is cancer, which we will address below. Genetic changes and reduced immune response with accompanying adverse consequences are also among the long-term effects.

Three factors must be known in order to estimate the number of fatal cancer cases due to radiation exposures. First, the average dose to the population over a given time period. Second, the number of people in that population. Third, the dose-risk factor which gives the number of expected excess fatal cancer cases (i.e., in excess of cancer fatalities of other origin) per unit of dose among a given number of people.

The method for estimating adverse health effects once the dose has been calculated is the same for both atmospheric and underground nuclear weapons testing, or indeed for any other radiation exposure.

The number of excess cancer fatalities can be calculated as follows:

---

1. Carter and Moghissi 1977, p. 56.

number of cases =

average dose (in rems) • number of people • dose-risk
factor (in cases per person-rem)

Similarly, the individual fatal cancer risk from radiation exposure
is calculated:

individual fatal cancer risk =

individual dose (in rems) • dose-risk factor
(cancer risk per rem)

The 1990 report by the Committee on Biological Effects of Ionizing Radiation (BEIR V), published by the National Research Council
of the United States National Academy of Sciences,[2] contains the most
recent data base for estimating the health effects of low-level ionizing
radiation and is based predominantly on data about Japanese atomic-
bomb survivors. In BEIR V, a linear, non-threshold dose-response
relationship is assumed. In other words, it is assumed that radiation exposure produces ill-effects no matter how small the dose, and that the
number of fatal cancers is directly proportional to the population dose.
The population dose is the product of the dose per person and the number of people receiving that dose.

BEIR V estimates that 790 excess cancer deaths (or between 585
and 1,200, with a 90 percent confidence level) will result from a 1-rem
exposure to each of one million people. Since BEIR V uses a linear risk
model, for a broad range of plausible doses it estimates the same number of cancer fatalities from a dose of one million person-rems, regardless of how this dose is divided. For instance, the method yields the
same estimate of 790 cancer fatalities among 50,000 people subjected
to 20 rems per person, or one million people subjected to 1 rem each,
or 10 million people subjected to 100 millirems each.

The BEIR V estimates of fatal cancers resulting from low doses of
radiation are, for solid tumors, three times higher, and for leukemia,
four times higher than those previously published by the same committee (BEIR III).[3] These increases result mainly from a reassessment of

---

2. National Research Council 1990.
3. National Research Council 1980. (BEIR IV [National Research Council
   1988] dealt mainly with the dangers of exposure to radon.)

doses received by the survivors of the bombings of Hiroshima and Nagasaki, which are now estimated to have been substantially less than previously believed. At the same time, additional cancer deaths have occurred among survivors. These two factors together produce larger risk estimates for low-level radiation. (It should be noted that the BEIR V risk factor was extrapolated from relatively high doses. The Committee recognizes that its risk estimates become more uncertain when applied to very low doses. Departures from a linear model at low doses, however, could either increase or decrease the risk per unit dose.[4])

The risk per unit dose may be revised substantially again. As the Committee points out:

> Most of the A-bomb survivors are still alive, and their mortality experience must be followed if reliable estimates of lifetime risk are to be made. This is particularly important for those survivors irradiated as children or in utero who are now entering the years of maximum cancer risk.[5]

Assessing the Effects of Atmospheric Testing

We will separate the calculation of the effects of atmospheric testing into two categories. First, we consider the effects due to the spread of fallout all over the globe, assuming a more or less uniform deposition over large areas and thus not taking into account hot spots far from the test locations or the higher exposures at or just downwind of test locations. Second, we consider the effects of local fallout on test personnel.

Global Effects

The United Nations Scientific Committee on the Effects of Atomic Radiation (UNSCEAR) limited its assessment of radiation exposures from fallout from nuclear weapons testing to the tropospheric and stratospheric portion of the radioactivity:

> The radioactive debris from a nuclear test is partitioned between the local ground or water surface and tropospheric and stratospheric

---

4. National Research Council 1990, p. 6.
5. National Research Council 1990, p. 8.

regions, depending on the type of test, location and yield. Local fall-out, which can comprise as much as 50 percent of the production for surface tests and includes activity present in large aerosol particles which are deposited within about one hundred kilometers of the test site, has not been considered in the Committee's assessments, as tests have generally been conducted in isolated areas.[6]

It is possible to calculate the expected doses integrated over various time periods and make an estimate of cancer deaths that result from all fallout by assuming uniform deposition within broad latitude bands. Our calculation of doses from global fallout takes this approach, yielding an order-of-magnitude estimate of the fatal cancers to be expected.

Local Effects

Though the number of people affected by local fallout was usually small, radiation exposure from local fallout was usually greater than that from tropospheric and stratospheric fallout. Thus, a certain part of the world population was exposed to a much larger risk than the average.

A few examples illustrate the point. The first U.S. test, conducted at Alamogordo, New Mexico, on July 16, 1945, resulted in deposition of intense fallout over an area about 20 miles from ground zero. Although the area was isolated and rural, the few people living there may have received doses of 50 rads. The result of the first Soviet test was even worse. The doses to the closest downwind communities *averaged* 160 rems, including internal doses. High doses have been reported subsequently for people downwind of the Soviet test site near Semi-palatinsk. (See Chapter 6.) The people of Rongelap Atoll in the Marshall Islands, the U.S. testing area in the Pacific, received a whole body dose of 190 rems as a result of the 1954 Bravo test, a 15-megaton hydrogen bomb.[7]

Dose Calculations

In order to calculate the total dose from atmospheric testing, the following radiation sources must be taken into account:

1. External gamma radiation from fission products.

---

6. United Nations Scientific Committee on the Effects of Atomic Radiation 1982, p. 212.
7. Lessard et al. 1985.

2. Fission products in the fallout cloud that are incorporated directly (by inhalation, for instance).
3. Activation products or induced radiation.
4. Plutonium-239 and other alpha emitters—these are especially important in the case of test personnel and in some hot spots.
5. Doses received through the food chain — this may be an especially important route for iodine-131.

The total dose from external gamma radiation due to fission products can be easily computed by integrating the expression for the decay of fission products in fallout discussed in the previous chapter $(R(t) = R_0 \cdot t^{-1.2})$ to yield:

$$D(t) = 5 \cdot R_0 \cdot (t_d^{-0.2} - t^{-0.2})$$

where
$D(t)$ is the integrated dose until time t in hours,
t_d is the time (also in hours) after the test that the deposition of the radioactivity took place in the particular location where the dose is being calculated,
                    and
R_0 is the dose rate expressed in rads per hour at one hour after the test.

This expression can be used to calculate the doses from fallout due to atmospheric tests and venting from underground tests.

Doses from carbon-14, plutonium-239, and other long-lived radionuclides are calculated by assuming a uniform distribution in broad bands in the atmosphere—a reasonable assumption due to the long half-lives of such isotopes. Doses from short-lived radionuclides like iodine-131 and sodium-24 are more difficult to calculate. The characteristics of a specific test, the activities and/or diets of people, and weather patterns downwind of the test all have an impact on dose. These variables are important for estimating doses received by people who participated in the tests or lived or otherwise found themselves downwind from a test. These difficulties are compounded by poor data-collection and record-keeping practices, making dose estimates less precise and more controversial.

Assessing the Effects of Underground Testing

The most important short-term effects of underground testing are those produced by venting of radioactivity. Once the magnitude of the venting is known, the calculation of dose can proceed in the same manner as for atmospheric testing. Fallout from venting is essentially like fallout from an atmospheric test.

The separate issue in underground testing is the radioactivity produced and contained underground. It does not contribute to dose via the atmosphere. Assessing the hazard posed by radionuclides deposited underground involves modeling how the long-lived radionuclides eventually find their way into the human environment. This is a long, difficult, and highly site-specific task, far beyond the scope of this study. We will consider two major aspects of the environmental effects of underground testing:

1. The cumulative amount of radioactivity left in the ground by testing at each location.
2. The prospects for containment and evidence of migration patterns, in qualitative terms.

Without knowledge of the specific design of each nuclear device exploded in the various weapons testing programs, we must make some generalizations about the quantity of plutonium-239 in these weapons. We assume that each weapon has a plutonium-239 component of four or five kilograms. Most weapons of the past two decades have used plutonium-239 rather than uranium-235 as the principal fissile element. (Plutonium-239 allows weapons to be more compact.) We will further assume that each explosion leaves behind about 2.5 kilograms of unfissioned plutonium-239. This is a conservative estimate—there is probably more.[8] Two-and-a-half kilograms of plutonium-239 is equivalent to about 150 curies. As governments release more information about the weapons that have been tested, it will become possible

---

8. This is a low estimate, especially for the weapons of the 1950s and 1960s, which were less efficient in their use of plutonium. On the other hand, some of the weapons used enriched uranium rather than plutonium, which would partly offset the underestimation. There are about 16 grams of plutonium per curie.

Table 1
RESIDUE AND HALF-LIFE OF LONG-LIVED
RADIONUCLIDES FROM UNDERGROUND TESTING

Radionuclide	Generation rate	Half-life
Strontium-90	0.1 megacurie/megaton	28.8 years
Cesium-137	0.16 megacurie/megaton	30.2 years
Plutonium-239	150 curies per test	24,400 years

Source for strontium and cesium: Eisenbud 1987, Table 12-2.

to compute underground inventories of alpha emitters more accurately.

Fission of uranium-235, uranium-238, or plutonium-239 results in fission products. These constitute the preponderant source of radioactivity after the nuclear explosion. The quantity of fission products is roughly proportional to the fission yield (in kilotons) of the weapon. Although total radioactivity decreases rapidly after the detonation, there remains a very large inventory of radionuclides with long half-lives to contaminate the surrounding environment.

Table 1 displays our assumptions about residues of three principal long-lived radionuclides due to underground testing and the half-lives of these nuclides.

To estimate the activation products from underground testing accurately requires information about the composition of the geological strata where each test is conducted and about the design of the weapon. For the sake of simplicity, we have limited our treatment of underground activation products to a brief and general discussion in the next chapter.

A more comprehensive estimate of long-lived radionuclides left in the fractured layers underground would include very long-lived fission products, such as cesium-135 and technetium-99, as well as activation products. Thus, our estimate understates the quantity of radioactivity that may possibly to be carried into the biosphere by water traversing the contaminated regions.

Chapter 3

GLOBAL EFFECTS

In this chapter, we consider the global effects of atmospheric and underground nuclear weapons testing. For atmospheric testing, we address the effects of what is officially known as "delayed fallout," that portion of fallout which "reach[es] the ground after the first day [and] consists of very fine, invisible particles which settle in low concentrations over the earth's surface."[1] In the chapters dealing with the specific testing locations, we take up "early fallout," which is deposited primarily downwind of test sites within the first 24 hours, and hot spots.

In the case of underground testing, we consider the total quantities of long-lived radionuclides left behind at the test locations, which pose a risk to the environment and to future generations. We have not made estimates of the worldwide doses due to venting of radioactivity from underground nuclear weapons testing. There is some indication that Soviet tests in particular may have resulted in substantial venting. If this is true and venting made a measurable contribution to global fallout, our estimate of negative health effects from global fallout will have to be increased.

We also mention tests in space—the region several hundred

---

1. Glasstone and Dolan 1977, p. 388.

kilometers above the earth.

Global Cancer Risk Estimates

In this section, we estimate the doses and cancers attributable only to the portion of fallout that is globally distributed. The dose estimates would be higher if local deposition were taken into account, but uncertainties about who was exposed to how much radiation would make these estimates far less certain.

From 1945 to 1980, 423 announced atmospheric nuclear tests were conducted, with a yield of 545 megatons, as shown in Table 2. Of these, 193 tests were carried out by the United States, 142 by the Soviet Union, 45 by France, 22 by China, and 21 by the United Kingdom.[2] Radioactive fallout was distributed globally, exposing the world population to an increased risk of cancer.

The UNSCEAR reports of 1982 and 1988 were used to arrive at the dose estimates presented here.[3] The 1982 UNSCEAR report provides an estimate of global radiation exposures from atmospheric nuclear tests. (The 1988 UNSCEAR report uses the 1982 assessment because more recent tests did not significantly increase the total dose to the world population from global fallout.)

To arrive at dose estimates UNSCEAR:

1. Compiled the list of atmospheric tests and their total yields.
2. Noted for each test that portion of the explosive yield contributed by fission (as distinguished from the thermonuclear or "hydrogen" component), because only the fission component yields fission products, which constitute most of the dose to the present generation.
3. Estimated the deposition of fallout in broad latitude bands, assuming uniform deposition within those bands.
4. Estimated the radionuclide composition of the fallout.
5. Made hypotheses about the pathways by which the fallout delivers doses to people (for instance, strontium-90 delivers doses internally, and cesium-137 delivers both internal and ex-

---

2. Because not all tests were announced, there are some discrepancies between Table 2 and numbers of tests reported in subsequent chapters.
3. United Nations Scientific Committee on the Effects of Atomic Radiation 1982, 1988.

Table 2
NUMBER AND ESTIMATED YIELDS OF ATMOSPHERIC NUCLEAR TESTS

Year	Ctry	Number of tests	Estimated yield (Mt) Fission	Estimated yield (Mt) Total
1945	USA	3	0.05	0.05
1946	USA	2	0.04	0.04
1948	USA	3	0.10	0.10
1949	USSR	1	0.02	0.02
1951	USA	15	0.50	0.50
	USSR	2	0.04	0.04
1952	USA	10	6.6	12.6
	UK	1	0.02	0.02
1953	USA	11	0.25	0.25
	UK	2	0.04	0.04
1954	USA	6	29.6	47.1
	USSR	1	0.5	0.5
1955	USA	13	0.17	0.17
	USSR	4	1.5	3.0
1956	USA	14	9.7	22.7
	USSR	7	2.5	4.8
	UK	6	0.10	0.10
1957	USA	25	0.34	0.34
	USSR	13	4.7	11.3
	UK	7	5.85	9.25
1958	USA	53	8.2	17.6
	USSR	25	16.2	35.2
	UK	5	4.54	7.24
1960	France	3	0.11	0.11
1961	USSR	50	25.4	122.3
1962	France	1	0.02	0.02
	USSR	39	60.05	180.3
	USA	38	16.5	37.1
1964	China	1	0.02	0.02
1965	China	1	0.04	0.04
1966	France	5	0.68	0.68
	China	3	0.62	0.62
1967	France	3	0.20	0.20
	China	2	1.72	3.02
1968	France	5	4.1	4.9
	China	1	1.2	3.0
1969	China	1	2.0	3.0
1970	France	8	2.55	2.75
	China	1	2.0	3.0
1971	France	5	1.95	1.95
	China	1	0.02	0.02
1972	France	3	0.12	0.12
	China	2	0.12	0.12
1973	France	5	0.05	0.05
	China	1	1.6	2.5
1974	France	7	1.1	1.1
	China	1	0.45	0.60
1976	China	3	2.37	4.12
1977	China	1	0.02	0.02
1978	China	2	0.04	0.04
1980	China	1	0.45	0.6
Summary				
1945-1962	USA	193	72.1	138.6
1949-1962	USSR	142	110.9	357.5
1952-1953	UK	21	10.6	16.7
1960-1974	France	45	10.9	11.9
1964-1980	China	22	12.7	20.7
TOTAL		423	217.2	545.4

Source: UNSCEAR 1982.

ternal doses).

6. Arrived at a global population dose estimate, taking into account population distribution in the latitude bands.

We applied the BEIR V coefficients (which convert population dose commitments to cancer deaths) to UNSCEAR's estimates of global collective dose commitments to estimate the number of human cancer fatalities caused as a result of that exposure. The results are shown in Tables 3 and 4. Table 3 estimates the collective radiation exposure to be 544 million person-rems (5.44 million person-sieverts) if the integration time for the collective dose commitment from carbon-14 is limited to the year 2000. Of the total dose commitment, about 18 percent is due to carbon-14, and 40 percent to cesium-137.[4] External radiation due to gamma-emitting radionuclides and ingestion together account for about 92 percent of the total dose commitment, while inhalation accounts for the remainder.

Calculating carbon-14 exposures over infinity and assuming a world population of 10 billion people for the millennia to come, UNSCEAR estimates the global collective dose commitment (which is the same as the dose itself in this case) at 3,044 million person-rems (30.44 million person-sieverts) or about 5.6 times the dose commitment delivered by the year 2000. (See Table 4.) Carbon-14, an activation product and beta emitter with a half-life of 5,730 years, delivers 85 percent of the total dose to the world's population over the thousands of years to come. Ninety percent of the total dose will be received by ingestion.

The average global individual dose commitment to the year 2000 is 139 millirems. It is dominated by cesium-137, a gamma emitter (half-life 30.2 years). Together, cesium-137, zirconium-95, carbon-14, and strontium-90 will deliver 76 percent of the total dose in this century. (See Table 5.)

Figure 1 shows cancer fatalities calculated using the estimates in Tables 3 and 4 and the BEIR V risk coefficients discussed in the previous chapter. Limiting the dose integration time to the year 2000, a total of 430,000 fatal cancer fatalities (between 320,000 and 650,000,

---

4. In Table 3, the integration time for the dose estimation is limited to the year 2000 only for carbon-14. For all other radionuclides, doses express total doses committed to infinity because the overwhelming majority of the dose from these radionuclides is delivered before the year 2000.

Table 3

ESTIMATED GLOBAL COLLECTIVE DOSE EQUIVALENT COMMITMENT AND ASSOCIATED CANCER DEATHS DUE TO FALLOUT FROM ATMOSPHERIC NUCLEAR TESTS, BY RADIONUCLIDE. DOSE INTEGRATION TIME UNTIL YEAR 2000. (ALL DOSES IN MILLION PERSON-REMS = 10^4 PERSON-SIEVERTS)

Radio-nuclide	External dose	Inhalation dose	Ingestion dose	Total dose	Dose in %	Number of fatal cancers — Best estimate	(90% confidence limits)
C-14		0.3	100	100	18.45%	7.9×10^4	(5.9×10^4 to 1.2×10^5)
Cs-137	150	0.1	69	219	40.30%	1.7×10^5	(1.3×10^5 to 2.6×10^5)
Zr-95	64			64	11.77%	5.1×10^4	(3.7×10^4 to 7.7×10^4)
Sr-90		3	44	47	8.64%	3.7×10^4	(2.7×10^4 to 5.6×10^4)
Ru-106	17	10		27	4.97%	2.1×10^4	(1.6×10^4 to 3.2×10^4)
H-3		1	18	19	3.49%	1.5×10^4	(1.1×10^4 to 2.3×10^4)
Ce-144	5	12		17	3.13%	1.3×10^4	(9.9×10^3 to 2.0×10^4)
I-131			11	11	2.02%	8.7×10^3	(6.4×10^3 to 1.3×10^4)
Pu-239		8	2	10	1.84%	7.9×10^3	(5.9×10^3 to 1.2×10^4)
Ba-140	8	0.07	0.05	8	1.49%	6.4×10^3	(4.8×10^3 to 9.7×10^3)
Ru-103	5			5	0.92%	4.0×10^3	(2.9×10^3 to 6.0×10^3)
Pu-240		5	1	6	1.10%	4.7×10^3	(3.5×10^3 to 7.2×10^3)
Pu-241		3		3	0.56%	2.4×10^3	(1.8×10^3 to 3.6×10^3)
Fe-55			3	3	0.55%	2.4×10^3	(1.8×10^3 to 3.6×10^3)
Am-241		0.5	2	3	0.46%	2.0×10^3	(1.5×10^3 to 3.0×10^3)
Sr-89		0.6	0.3	1	0.17%	7.1×10^2	(5.3×10^2 to 1.1×10^3)
Ce-141	0.4			0.4	0.07%	3.2×10^2	(2.3×10^2 to 4.8×10^2)
Pu-238		0.3	0.003	0.3	0.06%	2.4×10^2	(1.8×10^2 to 3.6×10^2)
Cs-136			0.02	0.02	0.00%	1.6×10^1	(1.2×10^1 to 2.4×10^1)
Mn-54		0.01		0.01	0.00%	7.9	(5.9 to 1.2×10^1)
Kr-85	0.001			0.001	0.00%	7.9×10^{-1}	(5.8×10^{-1} to 1.2)
Total	249	44	250	544	100.0%	4.3×10^5	(3.2×10^5 to 6.5×10^5)
In percent	*45.9%*	*8.1%*	*46.1%*	*100.0%*			

Table 4

ESTIMATED GLOBAL COLLECTIVE DOSE EQUIVALENT COMMITMENT AND ASSOCIATED CANCER DEATHS DUE TO FALLOUT FROM ATMOSPHERIC NUCLEAR TESTS, BY RADIONUCLIDE. DOSE INTEGRATION TIME UNTIL INFINITY. (ALL DOSES IN MILLION PERSON-REMS = 10^4 PERSON-SIEVERTS).

Radio-nuclide	External dose	Inhalation dose	Ingestion dose	Total dose	Dose in %	Number of fatal cancers — Best estimate	(90% confidence limits)
C-14		0.3	2600	2600	85.43%	2.1×10^6	(1.5×10^6 to 3.1×10^6)
Cs-137	150	0.1	69	219	7.20%	1.7×10^5	(1.3×10^5 to 2.6×10^5)
Zr-95	64			64	2.10%	5.1×10^4	(3.7×10^4 to 7.7×10^4)
Sr-90		3	44	47	1.54%	3.7×10^4	(2.7×10^4 to 5.6×10^4)
Ru-106	17	10		27	0.89%	2.1×10^4	(1.6×10^4 to 3.2×10^4)
H-3		1	18	19	0.62%	1.5×10^4	(1.1×10^4 to 2.3×10^4)
Ce-144	5	12		17	0.56%	1.3×10^4	(9.9×10^3 to 2.0×10^4)
I-131			11	11	0.36%	8.7×10^3	(6.4×10^3 to 1.3×10^4)
Pu-239		8	2	10	0.33%	7.9×10^3	(5.9×10^3 to 1.2×10^4)
Ba-140	8	0.07	0.05	8	0.27%	6.4×10^3	(4.8×10^3 to 9.7×10^3)
Ru-103	5		1	5	0.16%	4.0×10^3	(2.9×10^3 to 6.0×10^3)
Pu-240		5	0.02	6	0.20%	4.7×10^3	(3.5×10^3 to 7.2×10^3)
Pu-241		3		3	0.10%	2.4×10^3	(1.8×10^3 to 3.6×10^3)
Fe-55			3	3	0.10%	2.4×10^3	(1.8×10^3 to 3.6×10^3)
Am-241		0.5	2	3	0.08%	2.0×10^3	(1.5×10^3 to 3.0×10^3)
Sr-89		0.6	0.3	1	0.03%	7.1×10^2	(5.3×10^2 to 1.1×10^3)
Ce-141	0.4			0.4	0.01%	3.2×10^2	(2.3×10^2 to 4.8×10^2)
Pu-238		0.3	0.003	0.3	0.01%	2.4×10^2	(1.8×10^2 to 3.6×10^2)
Cs-136			0.02	0.02	0.00%	1.6×10^1	(1.2×10^1 to 2.4×10^1)
Mn-54		0.01		0.01	0.00%	7.9	(5.9 to 1.2×10^1)
Kr-85	0.001			0.001	0.00%	7.9×10^{-1}	(5.8×10^{-1} to 1.2)
Total	249	44	2750	3044	100.00%	2.4×10^6	(1.8×10^6 to 3.7×10^6)
In percent	8.2%	1.4%	90.4%	100.0%			

Table 5

ESTIMATED WORLD AVERAGE INDIVIDUAL DOSE EQUIVALENT COMMITMENT AND ASSOCIATED RISK OF FATAL CANCERS DUE TO FALLOUT FROM ATMOSPHERIC NUCLEAR TESTS, BY RADIONUCLIDE. DOSE INTEGRATION TIME UNTIL YEAR 2000.

Radio-nuclide	Total dose (millirems)	Dose in %	Individual cancer risk (world average) Best estimate	(90% confidence limits)
C-14	20	14.39%	1.6×10^{-5}	$(1.2 \times 10^{-5}$ to $2.4 \times 10^{-5})$
Cs-137	54	38.85%	4.3×10^{-5}	$(3.2 \times 10^{-5}$ to $6.5 \times 10^{-5})$
Zr-95	20	14.39%	1.6×10^{-5}	$(1.2 \times 10^{-5}$ to $2.4 \times 10^{-5})$
Sr-90	12	8.63%	9.5×10^{-6}	$(7.0 \times 10^{-6}$ to $1.4 \times 10^{-5})$
Ru-106	8.3	5.97%	6.6×10^{-6}	$(4.9 \times 10^{-6}$ to $1.0 \times 10^{-5})$
H-3	5.4	3.88%	4.3×10^{-6}	$(3.2 \times 10^{-6}$ to $6.5 \times 10^{-6})$
Ce-144	4.7	3.38%	3.7×10^{-6}	$(2.7 \times 10^{-6}$ to $5.6 \times 10^{-6})$
I-131	3.3	2.37%	2.6×10^{-6}	$(1.9 \times 10^{-6}$ to $4.0 \times 10^{-6})$
Pu-239	2.7	1.94%	2.1×10^{-6}	$(1.6 \times 10^{-6}$ to $3.2 \times 10^{-6})$
Ba-140	2.5	1.80%	2.0×10^{-6}	$(1.5 \times 10^{-6}$ to $3.0 \times 10^{-6})$
Ru-103	1.7	1.22%	1.3×10^{-6}	$(9.9 \times 10^{-7}$ to $2.0 \times 10^{-6})$
Pu-240	1.7	1.22%	1.3×10^{-6}	$(9.9 \times 10^{-7}$ to $2.0 \times 10^{-6})$
Pu-241	0.9	0.65%	7.1×10^{-7}	$(5.3 \times 10^{-7}$ to $1.1 \times 10^{-6})$
Fe-55	0.9	0.65%	7.1×10^{-7}	$(5.3 \times 10^{-7}$ to $1.1 \times 10^{-6})$
Am-241	0.4	0.29%	3.2×10^{-7}	$(2.3 \times 10^{-7}$ to $4.8 \times 10^{-7})$
Sr-89	0.3	0.22%	2.4×10^{-7}	$(1.8 \times 10^{-7}$ to $3.6 \times 10^{-7})$
Ce-141	0.1	0.07%	7.9×10^{-8}	$(5.9 \times 10^{-8}$ to $1.2 \times 10^{-7})$
Pu-238	0.1	0.07%	7.9×10^{-8}	$(5.9 \times 10^{-8}$ to $1.2 \times 10^{-7})$
Cs-136	0.006	0.00%	4.7×10^{-9}	$(3.5 \times 10^{-9}$ to $7.2 \times 10^{-9})$
Mn-54	0.004	0.00%	3.2×10^{-9}	$(2.3 \times 10^{-9}$ to $4.8 \times 10^{-9})$
Kr-85	0.0005	0.00%	4.0×10^{-10}	$(2.9 \times 10^{-10}$ to $6.0 \times 10^{-10})$
Total	139	100.00%	1.1×10^{-4}	$(8.1 \times 10^{-5}$ to $2.5 \times 10^{-4})$

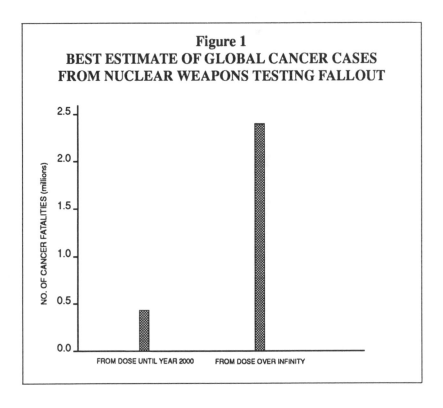

Figure 1
BEST ESTIMATE OF GLOBAL CANCER CASES
FROM NUCLEAR WEAPONS TESTING FALLOUT

with a 90 percent level of confidence) were and still are being caused among the world population as a result of global fallout. These deaths are and will be distributed from the late 1940s until close to the end of the next century. If the radiation exposure from carbon-14 is integrated over infinity, a total of 2.4 million cancer fatalities (between 1.8 and 3.7 million, with a 90 percent level of confidence) were, are, and will be caused by atmospheric nuclear tests. Because most of the exposure is due to carbon-14, the majority of the deaths will occur over the next few thousand years. Cancer incidence figures will be higher than the figures for cancer fatalities because some of the cancers will be cured and some of the affected will die of other causes.

The majority of cancer cases will arise from exposures in the northern hemisphere and will occur in North America, Europe, and Asia. Table 6 and Figures 2 and 3 demonstrate the regional distribution of doses, cancer risk, and associated numbers of cancer cases. Figure 3 shows that the average risk of dying from a fallout-related cancer due to exposures until the year 2000 is highest at 40 to 50 degrees northern latitude, with 180 cancer deaths per million (0.018 percent). This area covers the United States, Central Europe, and parts of the Soviet Union

Table 6

REGIONAL DISTRIBUTION OF GLOBAL CANCER DEATHS DUE TO FALLOUT FROM ATMOSPHERIC NUCLEAR TESTS, DOSE INTEGRATION TIME UNTIL YEAR 2000.

Latitude band	Deposition density (bequerels Sr-90/m^2)	Distribution of world population	Percent of global collective dose	Number of cancer fatalities	Individual cancer risk
Northern hemisphere					
80-90	260	0.0%	0.0%	0.0	1.5×10^{-5}
70-80	680	0.0%	0.0%	0.0	3.8×10^{-5}
60-70	1740	0.4%	0.3%	1.4×10^{3}	9.7×10^{-5}
50-60	2890	12.2%	17.9%	7.7×10^{4}	1.6×10^{-4}
40-50	3230	13.8%	22.7%	9.7×10^{4}	1.8×10^{-4}
30-40	2340	18.2%	21.6%	9.3×10^{4}	1.3×10^{-4}
20-30	1770	29.1%	26.2%	1.1×10^{5}	9.9×10^{-5}
10-20	1190	9.8%	5.9%	2.5×10^{4}	6.6×10^{-5}
0-10	810	5.6%	2.3%	9.9×10^{3}	4.5×10^{-5}
Southern hemisphere					
0-10	480	5.9%	1.5%	6.2×10^{3}	2.7×10^{-5}
10-20	420	1.8%	0.4%	1.7×10^{3}	2.3×10^{-5}
20-30	700	1.6%	0.6%	2.5×10^{3}	3.9×10^{-5}
30-40	760	1.4%	0.6%	2.4×10^{3}	4.2×10^{-5}
40-50	890	0.1%	0.0%	1.9×10^{2}	5.0×10^{-5}
50-60	470	0.0%	0.0%	5.6×10^{1}	2.6×10^{-5}
60-70	350	0.0%	0.0%	0.0	2.0×10^{-5}
70-80	220	0.0%	0.0%	0.0	1.2×10^{-5}
80-90	80	0.0%	0.0%	0.0	4.5×10^{-6}

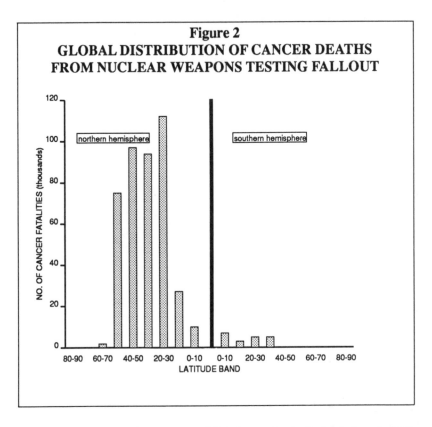

Figure 2
GLOBAL DISTRIBUTION OF CANCER DEATHS
FROM NUCLEAR WEAPONS TESTING FALLOUT

and China. Though the average risk is lower in the latitude band of 20 to 30 degrees north, the largest number of worldwide cancers, about 26 percent, will be caused in that latitude due to the large number of people exposed. (See Figure 2 and Table 6.) (UNSCEAR made one important simplification to calculate dose commitment until 2000. It assumed that the total population was exposed over the whole period, when in fact most of the population was exposed over less than the complete fallout period. Thus, the results reflect a maximum individual average.)

In summary, the fallout from atmospheric nuclear weapons testing has had and continues to have an impact on human health. The radioactive material that will be delivered to the world population until the year 2000 will eventually cause about 430,000 cancer fatalities, the majority of which will be in the northern hemisphere. The average risk of dying from a fallout-induced cancer is about 180 per million (= 0.018 percent) in the northern temperate zone between 40 and 50 degrees latitude. This must be compared to an overall cancer fatality rate of about 20 percent of all deaths. Thus, we can see that, although the total number of cancers estimated to be caused by nuclear weapons testing is large, it is dif-

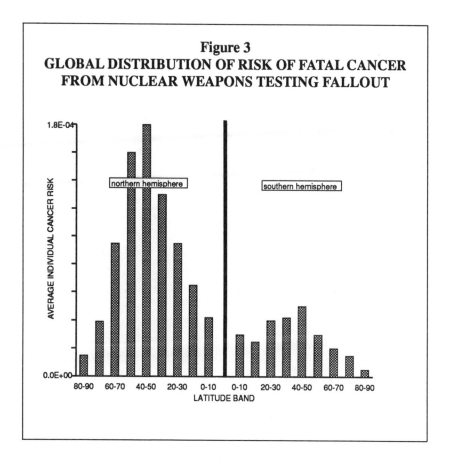

Figure 3
GLOBAL DISTRIBUTION OF RISK OF FATAL CANCER FROM NUCLEAR WEAPONS TESTING FALLOUT

ficult to detect those cancers resulting from global fallout because of the small percentage contribution to total cancers and the highly dispersed nature of the effect.

Considering the full effect of global fallout, most of the radiation exposure will be delivered over thousands of years and will be dominated by carbon-14 with a half-life of 5,730 years. The precise exposure depends on the size of the future world population, which in this case was assumed to be ten billion. Assuming a linear dose-response relationship, the total toll on human health will eventually be more than two million cancer fatalities.

These estimates of excess cancer fatalities are new, based as they are on the BEIR V risk estimates. As mentioned above, they are higher by a factor of three or more than those based on BEIR III.

Inventory of Long-Lived Radionuclides from Atmospheric Testing

The total yield of all announced atmospheric tests was about 550 megatons, including both the fission and fusion components. Because fission products result only from the fission component of the weapon, we must calculate fission strontium-90 and cesium-137 inventories from the fission component of the total explosive force of atmospheric tests. According to the UNSCEAR numbers cited above, the fission component of these tests amounted to 217 megatons.

However, the total number of atmospheric tests was probably greater than the number of announced ones, as the current estimate of Soviet atmospheric tests is about 210 (see Chapter 6) compared to the 142 estimated by UNSCEAR in 1982. We assume a simple proportionality between the number of tests and total fission yield. Thus, if the 423 announced tests yielded 217 megatons from fission, then we assume the 518 total (announced and unannounced) tests yielded 266 megatons from fission. (Note that, while the unannounced tests were probably smaller on average than the announced ones, it is likely that the fission component of the additional tests was close to the average fission component of the announced tests—most of the variation in overall yield of tests is due to variation in the thermonuclear component.)

The total strontium-90 created by these tests would be on the order of 27 million curies and total cesium-137 would be on the order of 43 million curies. However, since most of the tests took place in the 1950s and early 1960s, a considerable portion of the strontium-90 and cesium-137 has decayed away because the half-lives of these radionuclides are 28.8 years and 30.2 years respectively. Roughly 50 to 60 percent of the radioactivity in the strontium-90 and cesium-137 has decayed away, leaving about 11 to 13 million curies of strontium-90 and 17 to 21 million curies of cesium-137 on earth. Carbon-14 is the principal activation product from atmospheric testing, resulting from the transmutation of atmospheric nitrogen by neutron bombardment. According to aircraft and balloon measurements, the amount of carbon-14 produced by atmospheric tests is about 9.6 million curies.[5]

The following shows approximate estimates of four radionuclides (we include in our inventory all of the carbon-14 and plutonium-239

5. Eisenbud 1987, p. 334.

produced because the half-lives of these substances are about 5,730 years and 24,400 years respectively):

Strontium-90 . . . . 11-13 million curies
Cesium-137 . . . . 17-21 million curies
Carbon-14 . . . . 10 million curies
Plutonium-239 (4,200 kilograms) . . . 255,000 curies[6]

Inventory of Long-Lived Radionuclides from Underground Testing

There have been almost 1,400 underground tests during the period from 1957 to 1989 at various sites around the world. Underground tests have been conducted at nine sites in the United States and over 50 in the Soviet Union. In addition, France has conducted underground tests at two sites in the Pacific and at one in Africa, China has conducted them at its testing range at Lop Nor in Sinkiang Province, and India has conducted one test in Rajasthan.

The total yield of the approximately 500 Soviet underground tests is about 31 megatons, and that of about 730 U.S. underground tests is about 37 megatons (with both numbers rounded to two significant digits). The other countries do not add much to the total explosive content of underground tests, which is approximately 71 megatons.

The systematic and routine injection of long-lived radionuclides (fission and activation products as well as unfissioned plutonium-239) into the underground environment has produced an increasing inventory of radioactive substances. The possibility persists of serious contamination of another important segment of the earth's biosphere, the underground environment, where water is tapped for human use at ever increasing depths and in ever more remote areas of the world.

Assuming a fission yield of about 0.1 megacurie per megaton for strontium-90 and 0.16 megacurie per megaton for cesium-137, and unfissioned plutonium-239 amounting to 150 curies per nuclear test, we can calculate the cumulative inventories of these three long-lived materials underground. Assuming that about one-fourth of the cesium

---

6. Shapiro 1990, p. 394. Note that this number is based on data as reported by Shapiro, not on the assumption of 2.5 kilograms of unfissioned plutonium per explosion that we use in the case of underground tests, as discussed in Chapter 2.

and strontium has decayed away so far (since underground tests are of more recent occurrence than atmospheric tests, less of the fission-product radioactivity has decayed away), the decay-corrected inventories of the radionuclides would be as follows (figures rounded to two significant digits):

Strontium-90	5.3 million curies
Cesium-137	8.4 million curies
Plutonium-239	0.2 million curies

In addition to these three, there are substantial quantities of activation products, as well as other long-lived fission products such as technetium-99. To determine the total carbon-14 resulting from underground tests, one must know the nitrogen content in the underground environment, which is generally much lower than the nitrogen content of the atmosphere. We expect the carbon-14 resulting from underground testing to be correspondingly lower.

Silicon and aluminum, common constituents of soil, and manganese, an important trace element taken up by plants, form radioactive isotopes through neutron capture. However, their half-lives are only 2.6 hours, 2.3 minutes, and 2.6 hours, respectively. Therefore, they are not important sources of radiation beyond a few hours after an underground test.[7]

Contamination of Space

The United States has conducted nine nuclear tests in space, as high as several hundred kilometers above the earth. One of these was a 1.4-megaton bomb exploded 400 kilometers above Johnston Atoll in the Pacific on July 9, 1962. In addition to causing severe electromagnetic disturbances in the ionosphere and on the earth, it disrupted the Van Allen belts, which are bands of charged particles that circle the earth and interact with solar radiation. As a result of this test (as well as other nuclear events and debris in space), radioactive pollution has spread to outer space.

Although no other nuclear weapons power has exploded a nuclear weapon in space, the larger nuclear weapons exploded in the atmosphere injected nitrogen oxides into the stratosphere (the layer of the at-

---

7. Glasstone and Dolan 1977, p. 406.

mosphere between about 15 and 50 kilometers above the earth), where they catalyze ozone destruction. The largest atmospheric test was the 58-megaton test by the Soviet Union in 1961; the largest U.S. test was the 15-megaton Bravo test at Enewetak in 1954. However, attempts to measure and analyze the effects on the ozone layer of specific tests have so far yielded no results indicating significant or persistent depletion from the tests.

Chapter 4

U.S. TESTING IN NORTH AMERICA

The United States has conducted more nuclear weapons tests, both atmospheric and underground, than any other country. The global effects of atmospheric testing are addressed in the previous chapter, and we have also considered doses to test participants in illustrating the problems of calculating doses and conducting epidemiological studies. Thus, after giving a summary of U.S. tests, this chapter concentrates on four issues: 1) the location of the continental test site, which affected local exposure and hot spots, 2) the effects on downwind communities, 3) hot spots, and 4) the effects of underground testing.

Locations, Number, and Types of Tests

Through the end of 1989, the United States had conducted about 942 nuclear weapons tests, starting with "Trinity" on July 16, 1945. UNSCEAR lists the explosions over Hiroshima and Nagasaki as nuclear weapons tests, as we do here (see Table 2 in the previous chapter). (A major objective of these two explosions was to determine the effects of nuclear weapons—war-time commanders had been asked to refrain from bombing these cities with conventional weapons so that the effects of using nuclear weapons on them could be better evaluated.[1])

Of the 942 U.S. tests, nine were in space, five underwater, 203 in the atmosphere or on the surface of land or water, and 725 underground. The United States has conducted nuclear tests at 11 locations within the 50 states, at four island locations in the Pacific, in the open ocean in the Pacific, and over the open ocean in the Atlantic. Table 7 shows the locations and types of tests conducted by the United States. Figure 4 shows the weapons testing sites in the United States. The principal test site has been and continues to be in Nevada and is called the Nevada Test Site (NTS).

Selection of a Test Site

The United States conducted the first nuclear weapons test at the Alamogordo site in New Mexico during World War II, in preparation for the bombing of Japan. The environmental contamination that resulted was severe in some locations. The next two nuclear weapons explosions, over Hiroshima and Nagasaki, were also experimental explosions in a sense, as we have mentioned. Immediately after the war, tests were conducted in the Marshall Islands, to which we devote a separate chapter.

A great many of the effects of testing in the continental United States are a consequence of where the test site was located. For this reason, we reviewed U.S. government documents on the selection of the Nevada Test Site as the continental proving ground for nuclear weapons. These documents, some of which are quoted herein, provide insight into the interplay of military, political, health, and other factors in nuclear weapons testing and indicate a desire on the part of at least some in the military to show nuclear weapons in a more favorable light. This examination is only possible because many formerly secret U.S. documents have been declassified.

Testing at the Nevada Test Site began during the Korean War, but planning for the selection of a site in the continental United States began well before that. By 1948, the Joint Chiefs of Staff were seriously considering establishing a test site on the continent.

It was understood that there would be resistance to having a test site in the United States because of the public's fear of radioactivity. The

---

1. Makhijani and Kelly 1985.

Table 7

NUCLEAR TESTS CONDUCTED BY THE UNITED STATES 1945-1989

Location	Atmospheric tests	Underground tests	Total tests	Remarks
Pacific Ocean	4		4	2 underwater
Johnston Atoll	12		12	6 rocket shots
Enewetak	43		43	2 underwater, 18 barge
Bikini	23		23	1 underwater, 13 barge
Christmas Island	24		24	
Total, Pacific Area	106		106	
Nevada Test Site	100	714	814	
Alamogordo, New Mexico	1		1	
Carlsbad, New Mexico		1	1	
Hattiesberg, Mississippi		2	2	
Grand Valley, Colorado		1	1	
Rifle, Colorado		1	1	3 simultaneous explosions
Farmington, New Mexico		1	1	
Central Nevada		1	1	
Fallon, Nevada		1	1	
Bombing Range, Nevada	5		5	
Amchitka, Alaska		3	3	
Total, U.S. 50 states	106	725	831	
South Atlantic	3		3	rocket shots
Hiroshima	1		1	war-time use
Nagasaki	1		1	war-time use
Total	217	725	942	

*Includes 20 joint U.S.-U.K. tests at Nevada.

Principal sources: NRDC 1988, U.S. Department of Energy 1989, Greenpeace 1990 (for 1989 tests).

Figure 4

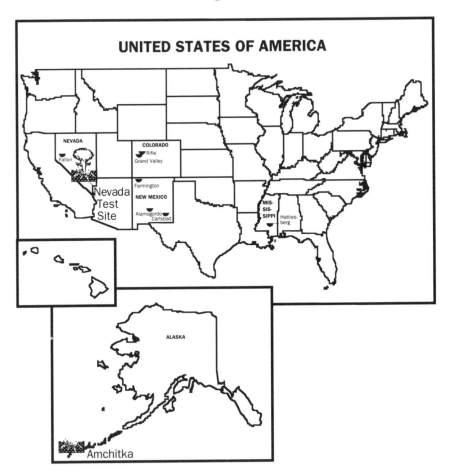

LEGEND

  Major sites of atmospheric and underground testing

At least three underground tests

One or two underground tests

"reeducation" of the public to take a more "realistic" and less fearful attitude was considered necessary in order to locate a test site in the United States. According to a 1948 memorandum prepared for the Army Chief of Staff:

> There appears to be a need for adequate education of the people of our country concerning the radiological hazards resulting from atomic explosions. This should be realistic in nature with the view to giving the public a correct understanding of this matter in order that the hysterical or alarmist complex now so prevalent may be corrected.
>
> ... Alleviation of their fears would be a matter of reeducation over a long period of time, and, until the public will accept the possibility of an atomic explosion within a matter of a hundred or so miles of their homes, establishment of a continental proving ground will be beset by substantial public relations and political difficulties.[2]

Further:

> The tremendous monetary and other outlays involved [in testing far away] have at times been publicly justified by stressing radiological hazards. I submit that this pattern has already become too firmly fixed in the public mind and its continuation can contribute to an unhealthy, dangerous and unjustified fear of atomic detonations. . . . Therefore, on a psychological basis alone, I believe that it is high time to lay the ghost of an all-pervading lethal radioactive cloud which can only be evaded by people on ships, airplanes and sandpits in the Marshall Islands.
>
> ... while there may be short-term public relations difficulties caused by testing atomic bombs within the continental limits, these are more than offset by the fundamental gain from increased realism in the attitude of the public.[3]

The Korean War accelerated the planning efforts, especially because the Army and Navy wanted weapons they could use in battle. Until that time, the Air Force had dominated the nuclear weapons scene. The Army and Navy were in a hurry to begin tests to get their own nuclear weapons suitable for field use. According to Bernard O'Keefe, Chairman of the Board and Director of EG&G, Inc. (a Department of Energy prime contractor), who helped measure the effects of many of the major bomb tests, including the 1954 Bikini hydrogen bomb test

---

2. Hull, undated but with attachments dated 1948, p. 3.
3. Parsons 1948, pp. 7-8.

Bravo and Nevada tests,

> ... an interservice dispute had arisen in the military. Atomic strategy, as it had developed at the turn of the decade, called for massive air strikes with high-yield weapons carried out by Air Force bombers. This left no nuclear task for the Army and Navy, who wanted a piece of the action, and fast. A war was going on in Korea; the Army and Navy requested small, low-yield nuclear explosives that could be delivered by carrier planes or fired from an artillery piece, so-called tactical weapons. The Defense Department agreed and laid a requirement on the Atomic Energy Commission for development and testing of such devices.[4]

The Atomic Energy Commission rose to the challenge:

> In view of the Korean situation and its impact on national war readiness, it is evident that increasing emphasis must be placed on the prosecution of the tests of atomic weapons now scheduled for the Spring of 1951. . . . [T]he results of the tests will have an important effect on the production of weapons for the War Reserve and on the development program for the thermonuclear weapon. . . . [I]n the light of present and anticipated developments at the Los Alamos Scientific Laboratory...it is more than possible that additional tests may be required for the same period.

> The Commission desires, therefore, to make known to the Department of Defense its strong feeling that there be no delay in the presently scheduled tests.[5]

In selecting the test site, one consideration was how to minimize the fallout over the country. Early on in the search for a continental test site, it was realized that practically the only locations in the continental United States that would ensure that delayed fallout would not land on the United States were in the East. According to a 1948 memorandum by a U.S. Air Force meteorologist, which was included in the above-cited military planning document for the Army Chief of Staff:

> Because the United States is predominantly under the influence of westerly winds, it seems obvious that the eastern coast areas of the United States may provide a suitable site. For example, the coastal areas of North Carolina are influenced by prevailing west to northwest winds to at least 50,000 feet throughout all seasons of the year.[6]

---

4. O'Keefe 1983, p. 148.
5. Dean 1950a.
6. Holzman 1948, p. 12.

The northern portion of the East Coast was ruled out because of potential contamination of the coast and of biologically rich waters:

> Meteorological conditions in the coastal strip between Cape Hatteras and Cape Fear are entirely satisfactory for removing the radioactive products, the winds aloft prevail from the west. The winds in intermediate and low levels can be predicted with sufficient accuracy to assure westerly components for removing radioactive materials from the test sites out over the sea. The same favorable wind conditions prevail all along the Atlantic Coast with more variability, however, along the New England Coast. Yet a grave disadvantage exists north of Cape Hatteras which does not prevail south of Hatteras. The coastal waters of the Gulf of Maine, Nantucket Sound, the south shore, the New Jersey, Delaware, and Virginia coasts, are moved by currents which hug the land. In addition, these waters are prolific with vegetable plankton, the principle food of the pelagic fishes. If "fall out" proves to be an undesirable quantity with regard to choice of test sites, all "fall out" can be avoided south of Hatteras, since the Gulf Stream flows from this shore toward mid-Atlantic.[7]

The site south of Cape Hatteras was rejected for one principal reason: the government did not own the land and did not want to wait to go through the process of acquiring it. Therefore, the choice was restricted to sites the Federal government already owned:

> There have remained for final consideration, after screening, the following areas:
>
> a. Alamogordo-White Sands Guided Missile Range in New Mexico (which contains the Trinity Area).
> b. Dugway Proving Ground-Wendover Bombing Range, in Utah.
> c. Las Vegas-Tonopah Bombing and Gunnery Range, Nevada.
> d. Area in Nevada, about fifty miles wide and extending from Fallon to Eureka.
> e. Pamlico Sound-Camp Lejeune area, in North Carolina.
>
> ... Of the above areas, the first three are partially or wholly under the control of the Department of Defense, on a temporary withdrawal basis, and permanent withdrawal has been requested by the Office of the Chief of Engineers. Since the fourth and fifth areas are not Government-controlled, and there are indications of some delay in acquiring the necessary land, they were also dropped from further consideration.[8]

---

7. Hutchinson 1948.
8. Dean 1950b.

Although data were gathered to find the site with the lowest potential fallout over highly populated areas, much less consideration was given to possible health effects than to logistical convenience. According to Gordon Dean, then Chairman of the U.S. Atomic Energy Commission:

> A geographical location as close as possible to the Los Alamos Laboratory, to enable accelerating the pace of the weapons development program is obviously a characteristic of such desirability that it could outweigh partial deficiencies in other respects.[9]

Ultimately, criteria such as proximity to Los Alamos and control of the site by the U.S. government won out. A test site in Nevada was chosen—despite the knowledge (clearly declared in the 1948 planning document) that prevailing westerly winds over any western site would blow fallout over most of the country and despite the fact that after the Trinity test Stafford Warren (Chief of Radiological Safety) had recommended that tests not be done in locations with human habitations within a 150-mile radius.[10] An official discussion team assessing the radiological hazards stated that beyond six to 12 hours "the fission products would be so diffuse that they could rain out without hazard," tacitly dismissing the experience of the Trinity test.[11]

Downwind Communities

Communities downwind of the Nevada Test Site received large amounts of fallout. The story of these tests and how they affected downwind communities has been told before, thus we retell just enough to give the reader a sense of how civilians were affected by U.S. testing, the extent of public health efforts, including dosimetry, and the extent of contamination, including hot spots. A lawsuit, Irene Allen et al. versus the United States of America, known as the "Allen case," provided much of the information.

The maximum permissible dose standard established by the Atomic Energy Commission (AEC) for the downwind communities during most of the atmospheric testing was 3.9 rads per year. However, in practice the onset of immediate symptoms of radiation sickness tended to

---

9. Dean 1950b, p. 5.
10. Warren 1945.
11. Reines 1950, p. 12.

be the dose at which action to limit exposure was considered to be necessary. The aftermath of "Shot Harry" in May 1953 provides an example.

Shot Harry, which came to be known as "Dirty Harry," released fallout creating alarm among the downwind residents. A public relations campaign was mounted, with the help of a Congressman, to calm down the population. Based on a comparison of the received dose to the higher levels of radiation needed to produce prompt radiation poisoning symptoms, people were advised that the doses were not dangerous. In other words, because there were no symptoms, the levels of radiation were not supposed to be dangerous. The details are given in a memorandum by Frank Butrico, an off-site radiation monitor:

> . . . Representative Stringfellow informed the group of his meeting with the A.E.C. people at Camp Mercury and that, from what they told him, there was no cause for alarm over what happened the week before. He was thoroughly convinced that every possible precaution was being taken to avoid over-exposing any of the communities around the proving grounds to excessive amount of radiation. He further indicated that the amount of fallout in St. George from Shot IX was not dangerous and A.E.C. gave him the figures to back their statements. He read these figures to the group and as a comparison, he quoted some levels of exposure that might cause radiation illness, which he obtained from someone with A.E.C. (I would guess the Advisory Panel). These figures were going to be released to the press and during a radio broadcast.[12]

This kind of campaign was conducted despite measurements that indicated dangerous radiation levels in the downwind area.[13]

Shot Harry was a clear example of how public education became so mixed up with public relations that the official goal of safety was largely subverted. According to Frank Butrico:

> We have taken steps as best we could with reference to roadblocks and people going indoors. We have many inquiries about people reporting they are sick. But anything more that we try to do, the more we try to disseminate more and more information, let's cool it. Let's try to get this thing quieted down a little bit because if we don't, then it's likely that there might be some suggestions made for curtailing the test program. And this, in the interest of national defense, we cannot do.[14]

---

12. Butrico 1953.
13. Butrico 1953.
14. Quoted in Fradkin 1989, p. 22.

At a 1961 meeting of the Atomic Energy Commission's Advisory Committee on Biology and Medicine (ACBM), an increase of acute leukemias was reported:

> Dr. Bruner reported on conversations held with staff of the U.S. Public Health Service regarding what at first seemed to be an unusual concentration of leukemia cases in the southwestern corner of Utah, roughly northeastward of the test site; this area had been subjected to early fallout on several occasions during the test.[15]

Although the minutes of the meeting go on to cast doubt on the finding, more recent epidemiological work has affirmed it. Walter Stevens et al. (1990) performed a case control study with 1,177 individuals who died of leukemia and 5,330 other deaths (controls) and used estimates of bone marrow doses computed from fallout deposition and subjects' residence locations. They found a "weak association between bone marrow dose and all types of leukemia, all ages, and all time periods after exposure" in the people living downwind of the Nevada Test Site. They also compared their results with those of other studies and found them to be consistent. The relative risk of leukemia as calculated by Stevens et al. was 1.72, with a 95 percent confidence interval of 0.94 to 3.12. The relative risk of acute leukemias for young people in the age group from birth to 19 (there was a total of five cases) was considerably greater: 7.82, with a 95 percent confidence interval of 1.9 to 32.2. The Stevens study did not evaluate the possibility of transgenerational risk—that is, exposure to one generation resulting in risk to the next generation, an issue which has recently been raised in relation to the British nuclear facility at Sellafield.[16]

The following are some examples of the gamma dose levels from some of the tests, as officially estimated. During the first shot of the Upshot-Knothole test series in the spring of 1953, official calculations for St. George, Utah, one of the downwind communities, "indicated a 460 millirads [gamma] dose for the inhabitants." Other locations in Utah received even higher doses: 2.1 rads at Rockville, 0.78 rad at Springdale, and 0.7 rad at Santa Clara. The estimates for the latter three places were each based on a single measurement.[17] Local variations within communities may have been considerable.

Because of a paucity of measurements relating to beta radiation or

---

15. U.S. Atomic Energy Commission 1961.
16. Stevens et al. 1990.
17. List 1954.

internal doses (see Chapter 1 for more elaboration), it is now a difficult matter to reconstruct them. However, we do know of instances where heavy beta irradiation occurred. The best-known example of this was the irradiation, accompanied by skin burns, of sheep downwind of a test in 1954, which was covered up by the Atomic Energy Commission until a decade ago. The shepherds took the case to court in the 1950s, claiming damages, and the Atomic Energy Commission falsely and knowingly denied that irradiation had occurred. When the case was reopened a quarter of a century later, the presiding judge, A. Sherman Christensen, noted:

> In such a setting it appears by clear and convincing evidence, much of it documented, that representations made as the result of the conduct of government agents acting in the course of their employment were intentionally false or deceptive; that improper but successful attempts to pressure witnesses not to testify as to their real opinions, or to unduly discount their qualifications and opinions, were applied; that a vital report was intentionally withheld and information in another report was presented in such a manner as to be deceitful, misleading, or only half true; that interrogatories were deceptively answered; that there was deliberate concealment of significant facts with reference to the possible effects of radiation upon plaintiffs' sheep; and that by these convoluted actions and in related ways the processes of the court were manipulated to the improper and unacceptable advantage of the defendant at the trial.[18]

The Department of Energy has instituted a project to assess off-site doses from fallout. The results so far indicate substantial exposures for downwind communities. Estimates of exposures depend on the assumptions used in computations. For instance, estimates of average exposures to external gamma radiation from the atmospheric testing program for the community of St. George, Utah range from a low of 2 rads, using film badge data, to 6 rads, using open air measurements, which assume no shielding.[19]

As part of this Department of Energy-sponsored reconstruction of doses from fallout, L.R. Anspaugh et al. have estimated collective external gamma radiation exposures to communities downwind of the Nevada Test Site. They estimate the total external gamma exposure at 86,000 person-rems, including 320 person-rems from ventings of underground tests during the 1963 to 1975 period. The estimated popula-

---

18. Quoted in Fradkin 1989, pp. 163-164.
19. Church et al. 1990, p. 508.

tion that received this dose is 180,000. Thus, the present official estimate of average external gamma dose per person is about 480 millirems.[20]

About 68 cancer fatalities would be expected due to such a collective external gamma dose, using the BEIR V coefficient of 790 fatalities per million person-rem exposure (with 90 percent confidence limits of 50 to 103 cancer fatalities). In addition to this, there would be fatalities due to internal doses due to ingestion and inhalation of radionuclides, including short-lived radionuclides such as iodine-131.

These official dose reconstructions are not yet complete.

Dose reconstructions such as those being conducted by the Department of Energy are based largely on data on deposition of radionuclides. However, as discussed in Chapter 1, the relation of deposition to air concentration as the fallout passed by a community depended on the weather and the sizes of particles in the fallout cloud. Particle size in turn would depend on the type and location of the test, for example, whether it was a test on or near the ground, a tower shot, or a shot farther up in the atmosphere where entrainment of dust would be low. Thus, estimates should be considered indicative rather than definitive. Also, none of the above estimates includes inhalation or ingestion doses. Inhalation doses calculated from deposition data would be particularly prone to error in cases where fine particles were present in the air but not deposited in proportional quantity on the ground.

The U.S. government has now recognized that the people who lived in Nevada, Utah, and Arizona downwind of the test site were irradiated during the development of nuclear weapons. Recent legislation sets up a compensation fund for some victims, though by no means all. The same legislation apologized to the people of the downwind communities for the injustices done to them during the course of the testing.[21]

Hot Spots and Other Environmental Contamination

There are many so-called hot spots in the United States—that is, areas far from the test location where deposition of fallout was much

---

20. Anspaugh et al. 1990, p. 529.
21. U.S. Congress.

more intense than in the surrounding areas. Perhaps the best known was in Albany, New York. The hot spot occurred during the Upshot-Knothole series due to a severe thunderstorm, which happened just as the fallout cloud passed overhead at an altitude of about 40,000 feet. According to the official evaluation of this test:

> An interesting example of a small area of very intense fallout occurred near Albany, N.Y., on April 26 following the seventh burst. On this date, the highest gummed film activity ever observed by the monitoring network, 16,000,000 d/m/ft2/day [sic], occurred on the film exposed at Albany airport. Although there are six monitoring stations within 150 miles of Albany, the fallout would have been underestimated by about *three orders of magnitude* in this area had there been no station in Albany.[22]

The official report on Upshot-Knothole estimated that a hot spot similar to the one in Albany over a location such as western Kansas might have had intensities of one billion to 100 billion disintegrations per minute per square foot at the time of deposition, five or six hours after the test.[23] This amounts to 4.5 to 450 millicuries per square meter, or 4,500 to 450,000 curies per square kilometer. Even short periods of human exposure to this level of radiation would mean that the dose received by such hot spot populations would be above the global average.

We have estimated the doses in such hot spots, as they would occur after the deposition of radioactivity, assuming deposition began six hours after the test. These are listed in Table 8.

There is a linear relationship between the amount of radioactivity deposited and dose, for any particular radioisotope. The actual dose delivered from fallout depends on the combination of radioisotopes; that, in turn, depends primarily on the time after the test at which the exposure takes place, since the short-lived isotopes do not play a role after a few weeks. The main component of the dose beyond one year is due to cesium-137. The dose on the first day, in contrast, is due mainly to external gamma radiation from the short-lived radionuclides.

It is likely that there was great variation within the hot spots themselves due to topography and irregular wind and rain patterns. And the hot spots that happen to have been detected may not have been the hottest ones.

---

22. List 1954, p. 63, emphasis added.
23. List 1954, p. 71.

Table 8
DOSE ASSOCIATED WITH HOT SPOTS
OF VARYING INTENSITIES

Period after test	Radiation level (millicuries/m^2)		
	4.5	45	450
Within the first day after the test (6 to 24 hours)	0.3 rem	3 rems	30 rems
Within the first year after the test	1.0 rem	10 rems	100 rems
Within 50 years after the test	1.1 rems	11 rems	110 rems

In addition to Albany, a number of areas received heavy fallout from the same test series in 1953. Salt Lake City had fallout due to dry deposition rather than to rainout,[24] and at almost double the level of Albany. Other affected towns included Ely, Nevada; Casper, Wyoming; and Grand Junction, Colorado—each of which had fallout levels of several million disintegrations per minute per square foot. These areas had levels of fallout ranging from roughly 10 curies per square kilometer to well over 100 curies per square kilometer. Airborne radioactivity during these periods was also elevated. For instance, a number of locations, such as Farmington, New Mexico and Winslow, Arizona, recorded airborne radioactivities of 100,000 disintegrations per minute per cubic meter (more than 45 nanocuries per cubic meter). Such levels were measured within a few hours of the tests.[25]

In addition to the large gamma doses, it is likely that many people who will never be identified received large doses of beta radiation to their skin and internal doses due to inhalation or ingestion during periods of intense fallout. In hot spot areas, children playing outdoors, and therefore possibly breathing heavily, would have been especially at risk of high inhalation doses.

---

24. List 1954, p. 7.
25. U.S. Atomic Energy Commission 1954.

Because of non-uniform deposition, atmospheric weapons testing produced vastly variable doses on the U.S. population. For instance, strontium-90 in milk in the Minot-Mandan region of North Dakota, at 33 picocuries per gram of calcium in August 1957, had increased to 105 picocuries per gram of calcium in 1963, four times the level in New York City at the same time.[26] Serious deposition incidents have occurred in many parts of the United States, such as Salt Lake City, Utah (75 microcuries per square meter); Boston, Massachusetts (25 microcuries per square meter); Albany, New York (80 microcuries per square meter); and Rosewell, New Mexico (65 microcuries per square meter).[27] Children who drank milk produced from cows grazing in these general areas received large iodine-131 doses, increasing their risk of thyroid problems such as hypothyroidism and thyroid cancer. In Nevada and high fallout areas in downwind states such as New Mexico, thyroid doses were probably on the order of 100 rads or higher. By way of comparison, the average dose in the northern temperate zone from all nuclear tests is 0.16 rad for adults and 1.8 rads for infants up to one year old. Other hot spots have occurred in New England, Nebraska, and Wyoming.

Biological incorporation of radioisotopes may amplify and prolong the variations in distribution of fallout. Strontium, whose biological behavior largely mimics calcium, concentrates in milk and bone. It may have its greatest effect on reticuloendothelial and hematopoetic tissue in bones. Both radioactive and non-radioactive isotopes of iodine are concentrated in milk and then in the thyroid. Children tend to receive larger doses of radioactivity from fallout than do adults, in part because of the concentration of iodine-131 in cows' milk. Milk levels of iodine and strontium have often been monitored in the United States.

Environmental Effects of Underground Testing

Here we address both atmospheric and underground contamination by underground testing.

Underground testing has often resulted in prompt releases of radioactivity to the atmosphere, mainly through accidental venting. In

---

26. Shapiro 1990, pp. 389-390.
27. Shapiro 1990, p. 390.

VENTING OF RADIOACTIVITY FROM THE BANEBERRY UNDER-
GROUND NUCLEAR TEST, NEVADA TEST SITE, USA, DECEMBER 18,
1970. The device, with a yield of 10 kilotons and buried at a depth of about 270
meters, produced a cloud of radioactive dust about 3 kilometers above the
earth's surface. After Baneberry, new containment procedures were adopted.
Photo: U.S. Department of Energy

the U.S. underground nuclear weapons testing program, it has been estimated that between 1957 and 1970, 25.3 million curies of radioactive fission products were released to the atmosphere from 30 underground tests. The venting of Baneberry alone, in 1970, injected 6.7 million curies of radioactive fission and activation products into the environment. Between 1970 and 1988, it has been estimated that 54,000 curies have been released as a result of 126 underground tests. Of 126 releases, four were containment failures, four were late-time seeps, 10 were controlled tunnel purgings, and 108 were "operational" (intentional) releases.[28]

The following is a list of some significant venting incidents reported by the U.S. Congressional Office of Technology Assessment (1989) (the quantity of radioactivity is normalized to 12 hours after the test):

Test name and year	Radioactivity
Platte, 1962	1.9 million curies
Eel, 1962	1.9 million curies
Des Moines, 1962	11 million curies
Baneberry, 1970	6.7 million curies
26 other tests	3.8 million curies

Underground nuclear tests leave behind a large volume of crumbled rock and radioactive materials. Assuming a total yield of U.S. underground tests of 37 megatons and that one-fourth of the strontium-90 and cesium-137 have decayed away, approximately 2.8 million curies of strontium-90, 4.4 million curies of cesium-137, and 110,000 curies of plutonium-239 remain in the environment.

The long-term dangers arising from wastes in the underground environment have not yet been carefully assessed. According to Eisenbud (1987):

> Whether underground accumulation of radioactive debris will in time prove significant as a form of environmental pollution remains to be seen. The quantities of debris involved are huge, but objective evaluation of potential long-range risks has not been possible because little of the basic data have been made available.

A more recent report by the Office of Technology Assessment, however, cites qualitative evidence of radioactive contamination of soil and groundwater at the Nevada Test Site. Although the full extent of

---

28. U.S. Congress, Office of Technology Assessment 1989.

contamination is not yet known, the report states that soil contamination at the Nevada Test Site is "documented and believed to be a threat to human health and the environment," and that groundwater contamination, too, has been detected. Radionuclides released to the soil include: antimony-125, beryllium-7, cadmium-109, cesium-137, cobalt-60, radium-226, rhodium-106, strontium-90, uranium-235, and uranium-238. Radionuclides released to groundwater include: antimony-125, barium-140, beryllium-7, cadmium-109, cerium-141, cesium-137, cobalt-60, europium-155, iodine-131, iridium-192, krypton, lanthanum-140, plutonium-238, plutonium-239, plutonium-240, rhodium-106, ruthenium-103, sodium-22, strontium-90, and tritium.[29]

The underground environment is drastically fractured by nuclear weapons testing. To gain a perspective on the forces involved, consider the following example. The United States conducted three underground nuclear tests on Amchitka Island, Alaska. The first, "Long Shot," in 1965, was an 80-kiloton explosion. The second, "Milrow," in 1969, was about a 1-megaton explosion to "calibrate" the island and assure that it would contain a subsequent test of the Spartan Anti-Ballistics Missile warhead. The third test, in 1971, was by far the largest underground test ever conducted by the United States, with a reported yield of "less than five megatons." This test was too large to be conducted in Nevada—the predictions of ground motion had suggested that an unacceptable amount of damage (in terms of claims and dollars) would occur to structures if the test were conducted there. Previous high-yield tests conducted at the Nevada Test Site had resulted in noticeable ground motion as far away as Las Vegas.

While the heat from the blast may produce some melting of rock, which might trap some radioactive materials as it cools and solidifies, most radioactive materials are deposited underground in a now highly fissured geologic environment, vulnerable to attack by water. As far as we know, there have been no official assessments of the doses to future generations that would result from this.

A worst-case scenario for an accident from underground tests at the Nevada Test Site has been developed by the U.S. Congressional Office of Technology Assessment, positing a prompt, massive venting from a 150-kiloton test (the largest allowed under the 1974 Threshold Test Ban Treaty). The release would be in the range of one to 10 percent of the total radiation generated by the explosion. Such an accident would be

29. U.S. Congress, Office of Technology Assessment 1991, pp. 158-159.

comparable to a 1.5 to 15-kiloton above-ground test.

In sharp contrast with the government-condoned unconfined releases of radioactivity from underground nuclear explosions, the criteria for isolation of high-level radioactive wastes that are being used to select and design the U.S. underground repository are relatively stringent. The U.S. Nuclear Regulatory Commission requires that the material in which the wastes are encapsulated stay essentially intact without any significant detectable leaks of radioactivity for a period of 300 to 1,000 years. Thereafter, leaks must not release more than one part in 100,000 per year of the remaining radioactivity. Even these criteria have been challenged as inadequate[30] because some of the long-lived radionuclide components of the wastes will persist for hundreds of thousands of years.

The U.S. Department of Energy has been singularly unsuccessful in its search for an acceptable site for a nuclear waste repository. After a 25-year search for a waste disposal site, during which many sites were supposed to be scientifically compared with respect to multiple criteria, the U.S. Congress terminated the process and enacted a law that restricted investigation for suitability to one site in Nevada. (Even this site, Yucca Mountain, is considered unsafe by some geologists who argue, based on the presence of limestone deposits, that mineral-laden water has invaded before and is likely to again before the radioactivity has decayed away.[31] Contact with water vapor or water might slowly destroy the containers and transport the radioactive materials into the human environment.) Yet right next to this site where the U.S. government is proposing extensive and expensive studies about containment of wastes, large quantities of radioactive wastes are being explosively injected into fractured underground cavities without serious concern about future containment of the long-lived radioactive materials.

In summary, more nuclear weapons tests have been carried out in the continental United States than in any other part of the world. Most of them took place in Nevada, a site chosen against public health considerations, resulting in contamination locally and across the continent. At the Nevada site, nuclear wastes have accumulated underground, and recent studies of a nearby location as a possible long-term high-level waste repository raise doubts about the geological suitability of the site and its ability to contain wastes over thousands of years. Thus, it ap-

30. Makhijani 1989.
31. Broad 1990.

pears plausible that some of the inventory of long-lived radioactive wastes from over 700 underground explosions will eventually reach the human environment, endangering people's health.

Chapter 5

U.S. TESTING IN THE PACIFIC

Locations, Number, and Types of Tests

The United States has conducted nuclear weapons tests at five locations in the Pacific, as shown in Table 9. In this chapter, we will consider the tests in the Marshall Islands. Christmas Island was under British control, and we discuss the effects of British and U.S. nuclear weapons testing there in Chapter 8. Figure 5 below and Figure 8 in Chapter 8 show the sites of U.S. testing in the Pacific.

Historical Context of Testing

Selection of the Marshall Islands as a Test Site

The Marshall Islands (Figure 5) were selected for nuclear weapons testing in part because of their remoteness. Situated in the Central Pacific Ocean, equidistant from Japan and Hawaii and just north of the equator, the Marshall Islands consist of 29 low-lying coral atolls (an atoll is usually a ring of islands and islets around an underwater volcanic crater that eventually becomes a partially enclosed lagoon as the

Table 9
U.S. TESTS IN THE PACIFIC

Location	Number of tests
1. Pacific Ocean	4
2. Johnston Atoll	12
3. Enewetak	43
4. Bikini	23
5. Christmas Island	24
Total	106

Source: U.S. Department of Energy 1989.

coral grows) and five single islands, for a total of 1,147 islands and islets spread over a sea area exceeding 1.3 million square kilometers. The total land mass is 181 square kilometers, with a population of approximately 36,000. Over half the Marshallese live on Majuro Atoll, the administrative district of the capital of the Republic of the Marshall Islands, and at Ebeye. The latter island is five kilometers from the U.S. base on Kwajalein Atoll and, although only 26 hectares in area, is home to 8,000 Marshallese. Over 5,000 people on Ebeye are from land-owning families evicted from Kwajalein when it was requisitioned for the U.S. military base. The remaining people of the Marshall Islands live on other atolls and islands collectively known as "the outer islands."

Aside from their remoteness, the Marshall Islands were selected because of the fear with which the U.S. public regarded nuclear weapons and, as in the case of the Nevada Test Site, because of U.S. government control of the territory. According to one U.S. military document:

> The preliminary planning for Operation CROSSROADS [the first tests after World War II] included a fairly exhaustive search for anchorages under U.S. control which would be suitable for conducting a test of an atomic bomb against an array of ships at anchor. Anchorages in the Caribbean and in the Pacific were considered including the Galapagos Islands (belonging to Ecuador). The only sites

Figure 5

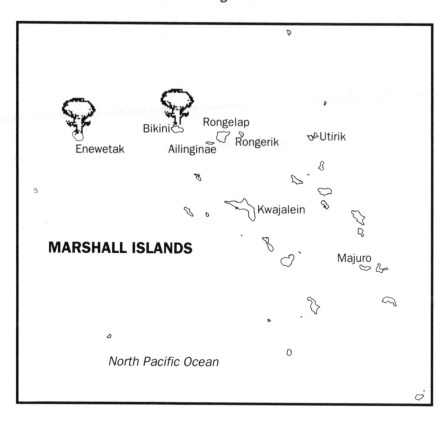

Bikini Rongelap Rongerik Utirik

Enewetak Ailinginae

MARSHALL ISLANDS

Kwajalein

Majuro

North Pacific Ocean

LEGEND

Atmospheric testing

which fulfilled the requirements for a good anchorage, free from violent storms, which would also permit heavy contamination by an underwater burst without seriously affecting pelagic fishes, were in the Marshall Islands.[1]

In the selection of the Marshall Islands, as with the choice of a continental test site, public health considerations were disregarded in favor of other advantages. A radiological assessment made for the U.S. Army Chief of Staff stated that the Marshall Islands did not "in the main" meet radiological safety requirements from a meteorological point of view:

1. From a meteorological standpoint, there are three basic requirements for a suitable site for atomic bomb experiments. These are:
a. There should be a reasonable frequency of occurrence of cloud or weather conditions to meet the operational requirements for the experiment. . . .
b. Wind conditions from the surface to stratospheric levels should be such that there can be no possibility of subjecting personnel to radiological hazards or surrounding land or water area to unintentional radioactive contamination. . . .
c. The mechanism of meteorological processes for the site should be adequately understood and the weather predictions for the site demonstrated to be of a high and reliable accuracy.

The Marshall Islands in the main do not meet these meteorological requirements.[2]

The actual experience of the 1948 tests at Enewetak (Operation Sandstone) bore out those observations, as noted by Colonel James P. Cooney, a radiological safety officer:

1. From a Radiological Safety standpoint, Enewetak Atoll has proven to be a far from satisfactory site for atomic tests.
2. The wind reversal, which usually occurred at twenty thousand feet, proved to be both a liability and an asset. An asset in that it caused a large amount of diffusion of the material in the cloud, thus fostering increased dilution. A liability in that the upwind fallout eventually reached the lower level winds and was then transported back over the lagoon.
3. The winds for both X and Y shots were ideal at the time of the shots, for maximum protection from fallout. However, fallout

1. Parsons 1948, pp. 4-5.
2. Holzman 1948, p. 10.

occurred over the entire lagoon during X plus thirty to X plus seventy-two hours, and during Y plus forty-eight to Y plus ninety-six hours. This fallout was insignificant insofar as personnel hazard was concerned, but was a nuisance and morale problem.

Due to the factor of delayed fallout the location of choice in the future for an atomic test should be a seaboard area where the winds retain a constant seaward bearing up to fifty thousand feet, thus transporting the radioactive cloud in entirety out over the sea. This would prevent this undesirable and virtually inevitable contamination of the area and material in the vicinity of zero point.[3]

These dangerous meteorological conditions, acknowledged by the U.S. authorities, were to play a tragic role in the lives of the people of several communities in the Marshall Islands.

The Tests

The United States began testing nuclear weapons at Bikini Atoll in 1946. The military governor of the Marshall Islands used Christian parables to convince the paramount chief of Bikini to abandon the atoll. On the understanding that experimenting with nuclear devices would "with God's blessing, result in kindness and benefit to all mankind," the chief told the governor that his people would be pleased to go elsewhere. The Bikinians were led to believe that they would be returned to their atoll after the tests were concluded. They chose to move to Rongerik Atoll, 200 kilometers to the east. This previously uninhabited atoll with only a quarter of Bikini's land mass failed to support an adequate diet, and by 1947 there were obvious signs of malnutrition among the people. After a period of dietary rehabilitation at Kwajalein military base, the Bikinians were moved to Kili Island. Although somewhat more suitable for growing staple foods, Kili has no lagoon and is frequently isolated from shipping by rough seas.

After two tests, the United States decided to move to Enewetak Atoll because it had a larger land mass and lagoon than Bikini. These features favored installation of the necessary instrumentation. Two series of atmospheric tests were conducted at Enewetak during 1948 and 1951.

Subsequently, the United States tested on both Enewetak and

---

3. Cooney 1948, p. 13.

Bikini, as well as at other locations in the Pacific. The first major thermonuclear device was exploded in 1952. It totally destroyed the island
of Elugelab in the Enewetak Atoll chain, leaving a crater in the reef 1.6
kilometers long and 300 meters deep. Testing subsequently returned to
Bikini and on March 1, 1954, the United States triggered its largest
hydrogen bomb ever, code-named Bravo, which was equivalent to
about 15 megatons of TNT.

In summary, between 1946 and 1958, several test series, known as
"operations," were carried out in the Marshall Islands (one series, the
1958 Operation Hardtack I, included three tests at other locations as
well):[4]

1946 at Bikini: Operation Crossroads, 2 tests.
1948 at Enewetak: Operation Sandstone, 3 tests.
1951 at Enewetak: Operation Greenhouse, 4 tests.
1952 at Enewetak: Operation Ivy, 2 tests, including the first
    thermonuclear test (10.4 megatons).
1954 at Bikini and Enewetak: Operation Castle, 6 tests, including
    test Bravo.
1956 at Bikini and Enewetak: Operation Redwing, 17 tests, includ-
    ing the first air drop of a thermonuclear weapon.
1958 at Bikini and Enewetak, Johnston Island, and a Pacific Ocean
    location: Operation Hardtack I, 35 tests.

The most seriously affected atolls have been evacuated and reset-
tled a number of times. The fears and controversies about residual radiation and contamination of waters and fish remain and, for some groups
of Islanders, have intensified over the years as more information has
become public.

Possible Resumption of Atmospheric Testing

The United States has a contingency plan to resume atmospheric
nuclear testing in the Pacific. This plan, known as "Safeguard C," has
been in place ever since the Limited Test Ban Treaty (which forbids atmospheric testing) was signed in 1963. In 1982 health and environmental monitoring programs for the Marshallese were transferred from the
environmental division to the military division of the Department of

---

4. U.S. Department of Energy 1989.

Energy (DOE). The rationale for this transfer was to integrate health and environmental research into a contingency plan to resume atmospheric nuclear weapons tests in the Marshall Islands.[5]

Safeguard C is still in effect. If implemented, tests are to be carried out over Johnston Atoll.

Downwind Communities

The extreme shortage of land, the fragility of the environment on which people depend for a living, and even the weather made the Marshall Islands an unsuitable place to test nuclear weapons. As a result of testing, the Marshall Islands sustained severe physical damage and radiological contamination. The people of Bikini and Enewetak were placed in exile by the U.S. government so that their atolls could be used to explode nuclear weapons. Other Marshallese were occasionally evacuated temporarily but for the most part were left on their atolls.

Acute Radiation Effects[6]

On March 1, 1954, Bravo was detonated as part of the Castle test series. The 15-megaton thermonuclear bomb was about 1,000 times more powerful than the bomb exploded over Hiroshima in 1945. Its cloud rose 40 kilometers and after 10 minutes had a diameter of over 120 kilometers.

Intense radioactive fallout from the cloud was carried eastward and severely contaminated a Japanese commercial fishing boat, the *Lucky Dragon,* and affected the atolls of Rongelap, Ailinginae, Rongerik, and Utirik. About five hours after detonation, fallout began at Rongelap Atoll. The fallout was so heavy that the Rongelap people, who had never seen snow, thought it was snowing. Children played in the radioactive powder. No warning was issued by the military.

Fallout consisted mainly of mixed fission products with small quantities of neutron-induced radionuclides and traces of fissionable elements. Radiation-affected persons were exposed to deeply penetrating whole-body gamma irradiation, to internal radiation emitters inhaled or swallowed, and to direct radiation from radioactive debris accumulat-

---

5. Roser 1982.
6. The main sources for this section are Conard et al. 1980, Adams et al. 1983, and Conard 1984.

ing on the body surface.

About 50 hours after the explosion, the Navy evacuated the Rongelap people. About 24 hours later, the residents of Utirik were evacuated. At the time of evacuation, the exposure rate at Rongelap Island was recorded at 1.2 to 2.3 roentgens per hour.

The 239 Marshallese who were said to have experienced "variably severe exposure" to ionizing radiation from fallout from the test were extensively investigated by U.S. scientists. Details were given in a series of reports and periodic reviews by the Brookhaven National Laboratory in New York and the U.S. Department of Energy.

The severity of acute effects was related to radiation dosage, being most marked among the 86 people from Rongelap, who received an estimated whole-body exposure averaging 190 rems.[7] This level of exposure, on the basis of current scientific opinion, is enough to result in a one-in-seven (additional) risk of dying from cancer. The estimated whole-body dose for people on Ailinginae was 69 rems and on Utirik, 14 rems. These are large doses of absorbed radiation. To give some idea of dose magnitude, the whole-body radiation from an extensive X-ray survey of the large intestine with contrast media would rarely exceed 0.5 rems. The dose from one chest X-ray is about 0.01 rems.

Initial symptoms were caused by radiation damage to mucosal cells lining the gastrointestinal tract. Nausea affected two-thirds of people from Rongelap, of whom 10 percent suffered also from vomiting and diarrhea. Five percent of those from Ailinginae, with intermediate levels of exposure, experienced nausea, and there were no gastrointestinal symptoms among people from Utirik, who had the least exposure. So-called "beta burns" resulted from direct exposure to high-energy beta emitters on the body surface. The result was reddened skin, sore eyes, and progressive hair loss. Caustic effects of highly alkaline calcium oxides from vaporized coral may have aggravated some of the external damage. About 90 percent of people from Rongelap whose hair became white with fallout ash experienced epilation (hair loss), whereas people from Utirik, where there was no visible deposition of fallout, suffered no external effects.

Hematologic indicators of radiation damage were closely monitored by U.S. officials. White blood cells and lymphocytes fell to half their initial levels in exposed people from Rongelap. It took, respectively, one and two years before the counts returned to normal. Blood platelets were reduced by one-third and did not increase to the normal

7. Lessard et al. 1985.

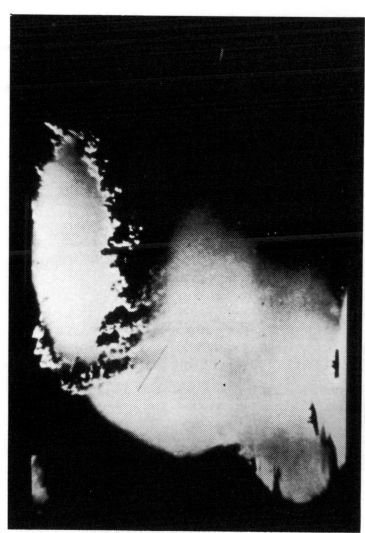

SHALLOW UNDERWATER NUCLEAR EXPLOSION, WITH FULL-SIZE U.S. NAVAL SHIPS, BIKINI ATOLL, 1946. *Photo: U.S. Air Force*

range for more than two years. Immunological studies suggested a temporary decline in immune competence. Ten years after exposure, chromosomal abnormalities were found in lymphocytes of half the sampled radiation-affected people—a finding similar to those observed in Japanese atomic bomb survivors and victims of other radiation injuries. An extensive survey of serum proteins failed to detect any instance of a variant gene product that might have arisen from irradiation-induced gene mutation.

Within days of the test, the 23 members of the *Lucky Dragon* (the Japanese fishing boat) also suffered from severe radiation exposure effects. Seven months later a crew member died, and the rest remained hospitalized under intensive care. The tuna aboard the *Lucky Dragon* were extremely contaminated. As it turned out, such contamination was not unusual. In 1954, Japanese monitoring programs showed that 683 boats had contaminated fish in their holds, with about 457 tons of tuna above acceptable levels. About one out of every eight inspected boats had contaminated fish aboard.[8]

The U.S. government has officially maintained that the Bravo fallout tragedy was an unfortunate accident due to an unexpected shift in the winds. It had been planned that the bomb cloud would be blown to the west and north, however, for unexpected reasons, the wind blew to the east.

Were the adverse weather conditions known beforehand? Dr. Merril Eisenbud, the Director of the Atomic Energy Commission's Health and Safety Laboratory, who also served as a scientific member of the "Bravo Task Force," recently wrote:

> There are many unanswered questions about the circumstances of the 1954 fallout. It is strange that no formal investigation was ever conducted. There have been reports that the device was exploded despite an adverse meteorological forecast. It has not been explained why an evacuation capability was not standing by, as had been recommended, or why there was not immediate action to evaluate the matter when the Task Force learned (seven hours after the explosion) that the AEC Health & Safety Laboratory recording instrument on Rongerik was off scale. There was also an unexplained interval of many days before the fallout was announced to the public.[9]

---

8. Lapp 1958, p. 178.
9. Eisenbud 1989.

Long-Term Effects of Contamination

Bikini, Enewetak, and Rongelap atolls were the most seriously contaminated areas in the Marshall Islands. The problems of restoring these islands to habitability and moving back the inhabitants have been controversial.[10] The policies at Bikini have been different from those at Enewetak, and both of these have been different from those at Rongelap.

The reasons for adopting different standards had to do with military preparedness, cost, varying standards, and possibly other considerations. We believe that a great deal can be learned as regards formulation of policy regarding clean-up of contaminated areas by examining the history and controversies that continue to dog this issue.

As early as the late 1960s, the effort by the U.S. government to restore the radiologically contaminated environment at the Bikini Atoll was designed not to interfere with military activities and, specifically, Safeguard C (the contingency plan to resume atmospheric testing in the Pacific). On February 11, 1969, the Defense Atomic Support Agency (now the Defense Nuclear Agency of the Department of Defense) and the Atomic Energy Commission (AEC) entered into an agreement for the clean-up of the Bikini Atoll, in which the AEC accepted the responsibility for "determining the radiological health and safety requirements" and the Department of Defense took responsibility for the clean-up. The ten-point, three-page Memorandum of Understanding exchanged by the two agencies refers to "treaty safeguards," and states:

> The Bikini clean up will not interfere significantly with the maintenance of the test readiness posture.[11]

It is not clear how this affected the quality of the clean-up, but the military was in charge, and activities on Bikini had goals in addition to clean-up. One benefit of the clean-up, according to the memorandum, was the opportunity to practice deployment of forces:

> The project will provide a unique opportunity for exercising the readiness capability of JTF-8 [Joint Task Force 8] in planning and organizing the deployment of men and equipment to undeveloped islands on short notice, at minimum demands upon outside resources, in a manner similar to that which would be required in support of treaty

---

10. Franke 1990.
11. U.S. Atomic Energy Commission and U.S. Department of Defense 1969.

safeguards if nuclear testing were ordered resumed in the environments prohibited in the Limited Test Ban Treaty.[12]

A later DOE memorandum confirms the overwhelming priority given to Safeguard C readiness:

> With the exception of professional medical capability, the technical resources that are in use in the Marshall Islands are largely weapons-related, and most of DOE's logistic and support base is common to the Safeguard "C" readiness program... [M]uch of the field effort in the Marshall Islands is an exercise of the expeditionary capability which is an important aspect of Defense Programs' Safeguard "C."[13]

Bikini

Pressure began to mount in the late 1960s to return the people of Bikini to their atoll. Since 1946, when nuclear weapons tests began, the people of Bikini had been living in exile. At the order of President Lyndon Johnson, the AEC and the Defense Department were asked to make the Bikini Atoll habitable.

The Bikini clean-up effort of the late 1960s relied on dose and risk assessment (estimates of exposure for people living in the cleaned-up environment), instead of maximum permissible radiation levels for every location on the island. Thus, "habitability" defined by the risk analysis did not ensure safety. When the people of Bikini were returned in 1972, it was understood that the consumption of locally grown food would likely increase radiation doses, but it was believed that if people were given advice on food restrictions and supplied with imported foods, Bikini would be habitable.

Unfortunately, these assumptions proved wrong. After several years, the internal doses to the Bikini people started to increase, and by 1978 the U.S. DOE was forced to reevacuate the atoll. Another effort to clean up Bikini was initiated.

Enewetak

In 1974, the AEC (DOE's predecessor agency) approved the first specific and comprehensive radiological protection policy for the Marshall Islands. It was established in response to a U.S. decision to return

12. U.S. Atomic Energy Commission and U.S. Department of Defense 1969.
13. Roser 1982.

the Enewetak Atoll, where numerous nuclear explosions took place, to the Trust Territory Government of the Marshall Islands. In September of 1972, there had been an interagency meeting to obtain agreements on agency responsibilities for clean-up and rehabilitation of Enewetak. From October 1972 until February 1973, the AEC undertook a radiological field survey of the atoll, published in March 1974. In July 1973, the AEC established a Task Group on Recommendations for Clean-Up and Rehabilitation of Enewetak.

Unlike either Bikini or Rongelap, the AEC concluded that clean-up of Enewetak had to address the problem of plutonium-239 contamination. There ensued a controversy between the AEC and the Defense Department as to the applicability of U.S. civilian standards to the people of Enewetak and whether higher dose levels for Enewetak should perhaps be allowed. In any event, the clean-up standards applied to Enewetak were more stringent than those previously applied to Bikini or Rongelap.[14]

Rongelap

The 1954 Bravo test (which contaminated Rongelap) sparked world-wide protest against atmospheric weapons testing. The issue became a major part of the public debate over nuclear weapons in the 1950s and early 1960s. In the wake of the major public outcry, in which several noted American scientists joined, the U.S. government's initial response was to try to downplay the health risks of weapons testing fallout. The U.S. government decided to return the Rongelap people to their homeland in 1957.

It appears that another reason the AEC was eager to return the Rongelap people to their contaminated atoll was that the agency was interested in studying how people absorbed radiation in a contaminated environment. In fact, in a presentation before the AEC's Advisory Committee for Biology and Medicine (ACBM) in January 1956, an AEC official noted that the people in the northern Marshall Islands provided a unique research opportunity because the area "is by far one of the most contaminated areas in the world," and

---

14. U.S. Atomic Energy Commission 1974, U.S. Department of Energy 1982b, and Franke 1990.

While it is true that these people do not live, I would say, the way Westerners do, civilized people, it is nevertheless true that they are more like us than mice.[15]

According to the minutes and transcripts of the meetings of the AEC's ACBM in 1956 and 1957, the Rongelap people were returned despite food contamination higher than acceptable for U.S. citizens and risks of congenital malformations from fallout.

Beginning in 1962, the people of Rongelap began to discover thyroid nodules. Over the years, 19 out of 22 exposed Rongelap children had nodules surgically removed. In addition, there was one leukemia death among this group of exposed children. By the late 1970s concern began to mount over an increase in thyroid cancer even among the people of Utirik, who were exposed to less radiation than the people of Rongelap. This concern was noted in 1977 by DOE's resident physician in the Marshall Islands, Dr. Konrad Kotrady. According to Kotrady:

> The theory was put forth that Utirik received low radiation, so a detailed follow up was not necessary. Now the facts of thyroid cancer at Utirik have strongly shown that the theory is wrong . . . It also further emphasizes to the people [of the Marshall Islands] that the United States really does not know what the effects of radiation are.[16]

In the same report, Kotrady also criticized the health care being provided to the Rongelap people in particular. The Brookhaven Program, which was supposed to provide medical care in accordance with federal law, "operates in a medical vacuum," according to Kotrady, and was primarily designed for research purposes. This corroborates a belief long held by the Marshall Islands people that they have been "guinea pigs" for the U.S. nuclear weapons program.

> The doctors always appear with a predetermined plan of what will be done, who will be seen and what will be achieved. The people are not consulted beforehand and are essentially ordered to do things... When the people raise any hint of an objection or seek to question some point, the doctors think they are trying to cause trouble. What seems to be forgotten is the patient's right to decide how, when, where or by whom he/she is treated. It is easy for a research project to neglect such patients' rights and feelings in the interest of the outcome of the program.

15. U.S. Atomic Energy Commission 1956, pp. 231-232.
16. Kotrady 1977.

Dr. Kotrady added:

> It is not hard to understand the people's point of view... [I]f an
> American was to go through this process each year for twenty years,
> would he also not consider himself a research subject—a guinea pig,
> if you will?[17]

Dr. Kotrady's admonitions about deficiencies in the DOE's medical care, health research, and the growing mistrust and resentment by
the Marshall Islands people apparently were not heeded by the DOE.

A crisis point for the Rongelap people was reached in November
of 1982, when the DOE released a bilingual report on radiation contamination in the Marshall Islands. A map in the report comparing the
radiological conditions of the atolls caused major concern. It indicated
that portions of the Rongelap Atoll appeared to be just as contaminated
with radioactivity as some of the areas in the Marshall Islands where
nuclear weapons had been detonated and where no people were permitted to live.[18]

By August of 1983, the Congress of the Republic of the Marshall
Islands unanimously passed a resolution asking the United States to
relocate the Rongelap people. In the following two years, representatives of Rongelap testified before the U.S. Congress, asking to be
relocated. The DOE asserted that Rongelap was safe but avoided dis-
cussing the map in the bilingual report. In May of 1985, a vessel
operated by the environmental group Greenpeace moved approximately 320 people from Rongelap to Majetto, an island in the Kwajalein
Atoll, at the request of the people of Rongelap.

The 1982 bilingual report had declared:

> If 233 people live on Rongelap Island and eat local food only from
> Rongelap Island, [s]cientists estimate that the largest amount of radia-
> tion a person might receive in one year from radioactive atoms that
> came from the U.S. bomb tests is 400 millirem. . . . The highest
> average amount of radiation people might receive in the coming 30
> years is 2500 millirem in any part of the body and 3300 millirem in
> just the bone marrow.[19]

This assertion was wrong for two reasons. First, the radiation dose
was estimated assuming that both local and imported food would be

---

17. Kotrady 1977.
18. U.S. Department of Energy 1982a.
19. U.S. Department of Energy 1982a, p. 39.

consumed.[20] If Rongelap people were to eat local food only, the "30 year whole-body dose" would be as high as 6.8 rems. This is above the 1960 Federal recommended limit of 5 rems over 30 years. Recently, a report by Lawrence Livermore National Laboratory[21] determined that doses for a diet labeled "imported food unavailable" were below the 1960 Federal standards.[22] The calculations, however, were arrived at by positing a starvation diet of only 1,256 calories per day, which is simply implausible (the U.S. Food and Drug Administration recommended allowance is 2,000-3,200 calories per day). The Rongelap people *were* on a "mixed food" diet in 1982, partly because they were afraid of eating local food, but the point is, were they to subsist on local food only, they would receive more radiation than stated in the report.

Second, the potential for exposure to plutonium-239, due to soil ingestion and dust contamination of food, was not addressed. The 1982 report determined plutonium-239 to be a minor contributor to the total dose, despite data demonstrating high levels of plutonium-239 in the urine of Rongelap residents from as early as 1973. Soil on Rongelap Island contains about 430 times the amount of plutonium-239 and other transuranics as the average for the northern hemisphere.[23] On the average, one gram of soil from Rongelap Island contains more plutonium-239 than a U.S. citizen carries in his/her body from worldwide fallout.

Measurements of plutonium-239 in the urine of Rongelap residents were made by Brookhaven National Laboratory between 1973 and 1983 and revealed alarmingly high levels.[24] These were dismissed as unreliable because of possible contamination with dust. The 1988 urine samples taken from Rongelap people now residing on Mejatto show much lower levels of plutonium-239 than measurements of urine samples taken in 1981 to 1983, indicating that contamination of samples by plutonium-bearing soil in combination with an inferior analytical method in use before 1984 may have caused the high readings of the past.[25]

One may wonder (1) why, considering that contamination of urine

---

20. Franke 1989a.
21. Robison and Phillips 1989.
22. U.S. Federal Radiation Council 1960, pp. 4102-4103.
23. Franke 1989a.
24. Franke 1989a.
25. Franke 1989b.

samples with dust was already an issue in 1973, a suitable sampling protocol was not adopted right away, and (2) why the Rongelap people were not informed about the problem until late 1988. As a result of these failures, the Rongelap people have little confidence in assurances by the DOE that the more recent data suggesting low body burdens are correct.

In response to the plight of the people of Rongelap, the U.S. Congress added a provision to the Compact of Free Association, an international agreement providing for independence for the Marshall Islands, calling for an independent assessment of the radiological conditions on Rongelap. The assessment was completed in 1988. It found that the northern part of the atoll should be considered "forbidden territory." Only when questioned by the U.S. Congress a year later did the study's author reveal that it would be safe for the people to return only if they could rely on imported foods for the next 30 to 50 years. However, the DOE currently maintains that its old scientific data are accurate and that it is safe for the Rongelap people to return.

Relocation and Clean-Up Policies

Observers of clean-up activities and the decisions about habitability have been struck by the inconsistency of U.S. policy. The U.S. Environmental Protection Agency (EPA) recommendations on exposure to radiation in the general environment state: "remedial actions should accomplish a permanent, rather than short-term, reduction in the potential risk to persons in the general population. Restrictions on occupancy or land use should not be relied on to provide the necessary protection to future generations."[26] Such recommendations have not been adhered to consistently and, furthermore, declarations about safety were not based on any firm technical standard and seem to reflect political rather than scientific judgements.

The radiation doses estimated by the DOE for the Enewetak and Bikini people, for example, were they to move back to their atolls without a radiological clean-up, were estimated at 1 rem over 30 years for residence on Enewetak Island in Enewetak Atoll[27] and 4.2 rems over 30 years for residence on Eneu Island in Bikini Atoll.[28] These doses

---

26. U.S. Environmental Protection Agency 1986.
27. U.S. Department of Energy 1982a, p. 64.
28. Robison et al. 1977, Part 5.

were below the limit in the 1960 Federal Guide.[29] The Enewetak people were not asked to move back to Enewetak, nor were the Bikini people asked to move back to Eneu without further clean-up of the atolls. At Rongelap, on the other hand, despite the DOE's own 1982 bilingual report indicating comparable contamination, no similar clean-up effort was recommended. Rather, Rongelap was declared safe for the people to stay there.

By way of contrast, at Johnston Atoll—primarily a military installation, which houses the chemical weapons incinerator, where no children live, and which relies entirely upon imported food—the U.S. Department of Defense applied direct environmental standards for plutonium-239 clean-up. The EPA clean-up standard of 0.2 microcuries per square meter of plutonium-239 or -240 was used, which is about five times more stringent than the one used for Enewetak Atoll and does not rely on site-specific dose estimates or risk analysis. All islands of Rongelap Atoll monitored in 1982 except Eneaetok have average levels above the EPA clean-up standard applied to Johnston Atoll. About 50 percent of soil samples from Rongelap Island show transuranics above that standard. Commercial clean-up of more than 100,000 cubic meters of soil will soon begin at Johnston Atoll, with a newly designed mining method[30] and a cost of $10 million.

Health Effects Due to Ciguatera

Nuclear weapons test explosions may contribute to ciguatera poisoning, which is caused by toxins produced by a small, single-celled marine organism (*Gambierdiscus toxicus,* a dinoflagellate) found in coral reefs. In an epidemic, fish that inhabit the reefs eat the toxic organisms and in turn are eaten by larger, carnivorous fish. The toxins have no observable effect on the fish, but when humans catch and consume them, ciguatera poisoning ensues. An outbreak of ciguatera poisoning often occurs after a coral reef is damaged. It is not clear whether the effect is due to an increased population of dinoflagellates or an increased production of toxin by individual organisms. Not every reef disturbance produces an outbreak, but a number of outbreaks can

---

29. In both cases, the dose calculations assumed a mixed-food diet. The possibility that only local food would be consumed was not considered in either case.
30. Kotrady 1977.

be traced to specific reef damage. Storms, earthquakes, tidal waves, and heavy rains are natural events that damage reefs, but in recent years greater damage can be traced to human activities—construction works, explosions, dredging, and shipwrecks. Since World War II, evidence has mounted linking ciguatera outbreaks to military activities and major construction projects that have damaged coral reefs.[31] Nuclear weapons tests may contribute to the problem.

Although rarely fatal, ciguatera poisoning causes a wide variety of debilitating symptoms, including nausea, vomiting, diarrhea, abdominal pain, trembling, and paralysis. Numbness, paraesthesias (alterations in sensation) of the lips and tongue, paraesthesias of the extremities, metallic taste, arthralgia, myalgia, blurred vision, temporary blindness, and paradoxical temperature sensation occur. In severe cases, there may be hypotension, bradycardia, cranial nerve palsies, and respiratory paralysis. Symptoms differ widely, even among individuals having eaten the same fish. The effects of the disease may last for weeks, months, or years, with persistent neurological symptoms: paraesthesias, itching, and loss of balance and muscular coordination. There exists no known cure or treatment that has proven effective and safe.

Individuals react more severely to repeat exposures to the toxin. Subsequent attacks tend to be more severe than the first attack, and eating certain foods, notably nontoxic fish, alcohol, or chicken, can induce a recurrence of ciguatera symptoms, as can the onset of another illness. Attacks of the disease during pregnancy may result in miscarriage or poisoning of the fetus, and ciguatera can be transmitted from an affected mother to her infant by breast milk.

Ciguatera poisoning has a disastrous effect on people who depend on fish as their major source of protein. Avoiding fish after an outbreak may cause malnutrition, especially among young children. Fear of poisoning also leads to increased dependence on imported food. In many Pacific areas, 90 percent of the fish eaten now comes out of a can.

The economic costs to the region are great. The development of fishing resources, which figures prominently in the economic plans of the South Pacific islands, is virtually prohibited in the hardest-hit areas. Subsistence and small-scale commercial fishing are the most disrupted because large commercial fishing operations are conducted farther offshore. Ciguatera episodes also force human migration from the outer

---

31. Ruff 1989a, 1989b, 1990.

islands as local food supply declines and the markets for potentially toxic fish evaporate. In all, the economic costs of evacuation, medical treatment, lost work time, and bans on the sale of certain fish are heavy burdens on fragile economies.[32] Moreover, publicized outbreaks hamper tourism, which is critical to the economies of many islands.

Ciguatera in the Marshall Islands

Fish taken from warm waters of the Pacific are known to cause occasional outbreaks of ciguatoxin poisoning. Among the islands of Micronesia, the sketchy statistics that are available suggest that the Marshall Islands have experienced ciguatoxin poisoning most frequently. In a 1982 survey requested by the World Health Organization (WHO) Regional Office, 56 percent of families in the Marshalls reported that at least one member had been poisoned within the last year.[33] Between 1982 and 1989, the reported annual ciguatera incidence rate for the Marshall Islands averaged over 300 per 100,000, more than three times the rate of any other Micronesian territory.[34] The most plausible explanation for a greater prevalence in the Marshalls is the extensive military excavation and construction and other activities related to the 66 nuclear test explosions at Enewetak and Bikini and at the Kwajalein Missile Range. Alternative explanations have not been offered.

---

32. Ruff 1989b.
33. Lewis 1984a.
34. South Pacific Epidemiological and Health Information Service 1974-1990, South Pacific Commission 1988.

Chapter 6

SOVIET UNION

Locations, Number, and Types of Tests

The Soviet Union has conducted nuclear weapons tests at many locations. The main test sites have been near Semipalatinsk in Kazakhstan and at two sites on the Arctic islands of Novaya Zemlya (Figure 6). According to the Natural Resources Defense Council, there are well over 50 other sites at which the Soviet Union has conducted nuclear tests.[1] Most of the tests away from the main test sites have been labeled "civilian" or "peaceful" rather than military.

The Soviet Union conducted its first nuclear weapons test in 1949. Between 1949 and 1989, it conducted an estimated 713 tests. Sources have differed on the exact number of atmospheric tests. UNSCEAR (1982) reported 142, while the Natural Resources Defense Council reported as many as 179.[2] The discrepancy is attributable to the UN's failure to include all the unannounced tests. Recent data from the Soviet

---

1. Cochran et al. 1989, p. 334.
2. Cochran et al. 1989, p. 332.

Figure 6

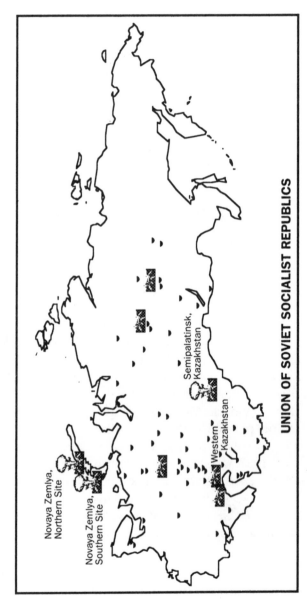

UNION OF SOVIET SOCIALIST REPUBLICS

Semipalatinsk, Kazakhstan

Western Kazakhstan

Novaya Zemlya, Northern Site

Novaya Zemlya, Southern Site

LEGEND

 Major sites of atmospheric and underground testing

 At least three underground tests

▸ One or two underground tests

Union indicate that the actual number of atmospheric tests may have been considerably larger—about 210.[3]

The Soviet Union's atmospheric nuclear tests include the largest nuclear explosion ever, conducted at Novaya Zemlya in 1961, 58 megatons, about four times larger than the largest U.S. test, which was a 15-megaton explosion in 1954. The largest underground explosion by the Soviet Union was of a 3.5-megaton weapon, exploded at the southern site in Novaya Zemlya.[4]

At least three of the Soviet explosions have been underwater, two off the coast of Novaya Zemlya and one in the Barents Sea.[5]

Table 10 shows the numbers of Soviet nuclear tests.

Table 10
SOVIET NUCLEAR TESTS

Location	Atmos-pheric	Under-ground	Total
Kazakhstan Test Site	120	347	467
Novaya Zemlya	90	41	131
Other locations	-	115	115*
Total	approx. 210**	503	713

Notes: *Announced as having civilian purposes.
**The approximately 210 atmospheric tests (conducted before 1963) include underwater tests.

Source: Thomas Cochran, NRDC, personal communication, October 18, 1990.

---

3. Thomas Cochran, personal communication, October 18, 1990.
4. Cochran et al. 1989, p. 335.
5. Thomas Cochran, personal communication, October 18, 1990.

Historical Context of Testing

The Soviet Union began nuclear testing in 1949. The first Soviet test of a thermonuclear weapon was in 1953, one year after the first U.S. test of such a weapon. However, in the early years the Soviet Union conducted far fewer nuclear weapons tests than did the United States.

Various official and unofficial scientific bodies in the Soviet Union have begun to make estimates of doses to downwind communities that give the strong impression that health and environment were neglected in the testing program. Such neglect has also been clearly indicated by anecdotal information we gathered from people who worked in the nuclear weapons programs or from people who lived near the test sites—no one remembers much concern for the health of people or for the environment.

There was a hiatus in testing from November 1958 until September 1961, when the Soviet Union and the United States had a bilateral moratorium on testing. But when Soviet testing resumed, it was at a faster pace and with bigger weapons. In 1961, the year of the Berlin crisis, the Soviets tested a 58-megaton thermonuclear device above ground at the northern site in Novaya Zemlya. This was the largest-yield device ever exploded. The following year, the year of the Cuban missile crisis, also saw a large number of atmospheric tests.

Downwind Communities

Despite the advent of *glasnost,* much about the Soviet nuclear weapons program remains secret. We have several Soviet documents about exposures to communities downwind of the test site near Semipalatinsk in Kazakhstan but considerably less information about Novaya Zemlya. Interviews with residents added anecdotal evidence. On exposures to communities at other sites, we have no official or even unofficial scientific data. Nor do we have data on exposures to personnel who participated in the tests.

The currently available data, to the extent they are accurate, permit us to draw some preliminary conclusions about the Soviet nuclear weapons testing program and its effect on downwind communities. The early evidence regarding the nuclear weapons production complex and conditions at the Kazakhstan test site point toward heavy exposure to workers and people in downwind communities. A full evaluation must, however, await the release of additional data. After reviewing the available information about the downwind communities in Kazakhstan, we take a brief look at Novaya Zemlya.

Kazakhstan: Doses and Cancer Fatalities

A body of literature is emerging about doses and health effects on the communities downwind of the Kazakhstan test site. The reports are incomplete and reflect many perspectives. However, no one challenges the conclusion that many people were heavily exposed.

The information we have obtained permits us to analyze the implications of the observed or estimated doses in terms of cancer fatalities. However, it should be noted that we do not have the original documentation for any of the data that are now emerging. The sources of data are inadequately described and we do not know whether these reports were subjected to rigorous scientific review. Given that we have neither the official raw data nor any body of scientific literature into which these data have been incorporated, it is difficult to assess the quality of the information presented here and, hence, the quality of the results based on that information. There are some discrepancies and problems with the data, which we will discuss.

One way to determine the total radiation dose to the population is to determine the cancer rate in the population. The excess over the expected is equal to the rate attributed to nuclear weapons testing. Then, using BEIR V estimates, the dose required to cause such an increase can be calculated. In the Soviet case there are three different cancer rate estimates available to us. The first is from the Tsyb Commission's work.

In May 1989, the Soviet Council of Ministers appointed a commission consisting of 70 government scientists to examine the health and ecological situation at the Kazakhstan test site. The commission was headed by Academician A.F. Tsyb, Director of the Scientific Research Institute of Medical Radiology of the USSR Academy of Medical Sciences. We refer to the commission as the Tsyb Commission.

The Tsyb Commission came to the following conclusion regarding doses to the downwind population:

It has been established that in the functioning of the test site during forty years, two periods can be singled out considerably differing in volume of radiation impact . . .: the period of ground and atmospheric testing (1949-1963) and the period of underground tests (1963-1989). Collective doses of irradiation . . . were received mainly in the period from 1949 (the first atomic test) to 1953 (the first explosion of hydrogen bomb). The greatest radiation impact of external and internal radiation was felt by residents of the populated centers in the Abai, Beskaragay and Zhanasemey districts of the Semipalatinsk region.[6]

The Tsyb Commission identified the following communities within these areas as being the most heavily affected: Dolon (876 people), Kainar (1,930 people), Sarzhal (159 people), Karaul (1,620 people), Semyonovka (1,690 people).[7] The dates at which these populations were estimated are not specified.

In all, the Tsyb Commission estimated that 10,000 residents of the region received the "main part of the collective dose." Doses were estimated as follows:

> The volume of average effective doses, with due consideration of external and internal irradiation by maximal standards, are respectively [for the above communities] as follows: 160 rem (the result of [the] 1949 explosion), 24 rem, 20 [rem], 37 [rem] and two rem. The greatest annual dose was received by residents of Semipalatinsk in [the] 1954 -1958 [period]—0.56 rem with the population being about 140,000 people.[8]

The Tsyb Commission failed to provide much help in understanding its analysis, at least in the incomplete documentation we have. It does not, for example, provide information about the dose-response assumptions used in making estimates. Nor does the report provide any of the raw data or the sources of data upon which it relied for making the dose estimates. The only relevant piece of technical information in the documents we have is that iodine-131 and strontium-90 were considered to be the principal vehicles for internal doses. (However, this is an insufficient basis for calculating internal doses, as normally internal doses from cesium-137 are also significant.) Plutonium-239 contamination is apparently not discussed by the Tsyb Commission.

The Tsyb Commission estimated that the radiation doses to the 10,000 people in the exposed group receiving 10 rads or less would result in 55 additional cancer cases during a period of 40 years, compared to an expected 824 cases of "spontaneous," non-radiogenic cancers. Thus, the increase in cancer incidence to the group was estimated to be about 7 percent. The Tsyb Commission estimated that the people of the Semipalatinsk region would suffer an additional 16 cases of cancer attributable to nuclear weapons tests.

---

6. Tsyb Commission 1989, p. 7.
7. Tsyb Commission 1989.
8. Tsyb Commission 1989.

The second set of data available to us was from a Kazakh cancer researcher. At the European Regional Meeting of International Physicians for the Prevention of Nuclear War in 1990, Professor Saim Balmukhanov, Deputy Director of the Kazakhstan Oncology Institute, presented estimates of the number of people at risk that were much larger than those of the Tsyb Commission. Table 11 shows the data presented by Balmukhanov[9] and by the Tsyb Commission:

Table 11 TWO ESTIMATES OF POPULATION EXPOSURES TO RADIOACTIVITY IN KAZAKHSTAN		
Average dose (rads)	**Estimate of number of people exposed**	
	Balmukhanov	**Tsyb Commission**
10 or less	100,000-200,000	10,000
160	30,000-40,000	1,000
280	1,000 in Dolon	?

From these data, the Tsyb Commission population dose would be on the order of 200,000 rems, spread over a population of 11,000 people. According to the BEIR V coefficients, this would yield about 160 additional cancer fatalities.

If one assumes that the exposed population was as proposed by Balmukhanov, the population doses amount to approximately 5.6 to 7.7 million rems to a population of 130,000 to 240,000. This means about 4,400 to 6,100 additional cancer fatalities, or an increase in the cancer risk from all sources of 13 to 17 percent. The lower figure is comparable to the Tsyb Commission's risk estimate, but applied to a much larger population. Balmukanov's estimate that 30,000 to 40,000 people received an average dose of as much as 160 rems would lead to an approximate doubling of the cancer risk (compared to "normal") in that population.

The third data set comes from a report prepared by a commission

---

9. Balmukhanov 1990.

DIRECTOR OF KAZAKHSTAN TEST SITE ADDRESSING JOURNALISTS.   *Photo by Yuri Kuidin*

created by the USSR Congress of People's Deputies which found that cancer death rates among the 10,000 most highly exposed people were 39 percent above expected:

> According to a report of Dr. B. Gusev, chief physician of the polyclinic No. 4 in Semipalatinsk, two major groups of the local population were examined and studied starting in 1961. The first, main group, consisted of 10,000 people who were exposed to radiation. The second, control group, also of 10,000 people, was selected from the same residential areas as the main group. Altogether there are 13 residential areas out of 40 contaminated areas which are under the study of specialists. The study showed that over 27 years the death rate due to cancerous diseases in the exposed group was 39 percent higher than in the control group.[10]

How can one reconcile these data? The 7 percent increase in cancer incidence described by the Tsyb Commission is lower than results obtained by working backwards from either Balmukhanov's or the People's Deputies' Commission's results. To get a 39 percent increase in cancer incidence, using recent BEIR V multipliers, 10,000 people would have to have received about 630,000 rems; in other words, the average dose per person would have to have been 63 rems. This is more consistent with Balmukhanov's dose estimate but spread over a population one-third to one-fourth the size.

(In the above calculations of relative risk, we have assumed a cancer fatality rate of 20 percent from causes other than radiation from nuclear testing.)

The other more limited studies available to us describe doses that fall within the very broad dose range of the above studies. They also provide estimates of iodine-131 doses to the thyroid. Dr. Tanibergen Tokhtarov, the head of the Kazakh Parliament's Committee on Health Protection, estimated that whole-body external gamma radiation doses to the downwind population from the very first Soviet nuclear weapons test were 160 to 200 rems in the first month. He further estimated doses to the thyroid gland at 130 rems. These estimates do not accord with data from other areas about the relationship of the whole-body gamma dose to the thyroid dose.[11] For example, the whole-body dose received by the people of Rongelap was about the same as that proposed for downwind Kazakhs. However, the thyroid dose at Rongelap ranged

---

10. Commission of People's Deputies 1990.
11. Tokhtarov 1990.

from a high of 5,200 rems for a one-year-old child to 1,200 rems for an adult. These are an order-of-magnitude or more greater than the thyroid dose estimate provided by Tokhtarov. Diet can only explain a portion of this difference, and environmental measurements from subsequent tests provided below suggest that Tokhtarov's thyroid dose is an underestimate.

Tokhtarov also gives estimates of exposures from other tests. For instance, he cites a radiation level of 40 to 60 milliroentgens per hour in some villages near the Kazakhstan test site on the ninth day after the first Soviet thermonuclear explosion in 1953. People were evacuated from these villages during the test but allowed to return home on the ninth day. Tokhtarov's estimate of the integrated dose from this test to the most exposed downwind communities is 37 to 42 rems, including both internal and external radiation.[12] According to Tokhtarov, the limit placed on radiation exposure to the downwind population was as high as 50 rems per year.[13] (By way of comparison, current U.S. standards limit the dose to the general public to 0.5 rems per year—100 times less—and the current Soviet standard is 35 rems over a lifetime.)

In conclusion, radiation doses to ten thousand or more people downwind of the Kazakhstan test site were in all likelihood very high. There appears to be evidence of an increase in cancer rate at least among some of the population. However, given preliminary reports coming from diverse sources, it is impossible to judge the accuracy or validity of the estimates. An examination of the raw data and the record-keeping practices during the atmospheric testing period would be needed to get a better assessment of the radiation doses received by the downwind communities. The true effect on health may be even more difficult to sort out because uncertainties in radiation-related data are compounded by inadequacies in data on general health status, probably precluding the selection of an appropriate control group.

Kazakhstan: Health Effects Other Than Cancer

The Tsyb Commission subjected samples collected from 98 people in the highly exposed risk group to cytologic examinations. It concluded that:

---

12. Tokhtarov 1990.
13. Tokhtarov 1990.

Persons subjected to radiation impact during the ground and atmospheric tests showed [a] predominance of aberrations of the chromosomic type with the presence of complex structural changes on the background of the general increase in their incidence.[14]

The Tsyb Commission also noted chromosomal changes in the "control group" it selected. These were ascribed to chemical mutagens, illustrating the problem of selecting appropriate control groups for study of health effects from radiation.

The Commission of People's Deputies made the following observations about health effects other than cancer:

- the average life expectancy in the oblast [region] decreased by three years compared with 1970;
- a certain increase by 1.5 to 4.5 times of the average spontaneous level of chromosomic changes in the lymphocytes of the peripheral blood system was detected;
- 40 to 50 percent of the examined people showed a decrease in immunological status down to the lowest level of the norm;
- from 1986 to 1988 the birth defects in children increased from 6.4 percent to 8.6 percent. Fatal birth defects increased from 2.3 percent to 7.3 percent;
- there was a steady growth in cases of nervous disorder among children suffering from mental retardation;
- the analysis of the situation in the areas adjacent to the test site showed an increase in suicides by 2.5 times compared with all Soviet Union averages;
- every nuclear test caused a dramatic increase in the number of people seeking help at local medical facilities of the city and oblast
  . . .

According to a commission led by corresponding member of the Academy of Medical Sciences, Acad. A. Tsyb, the nuclear test site in Semipalatinsk appears to be a traumatizing factor very negatively affecting the psychological health of the population . . .

There are reliable data available to prove that children of the second generation of atomic test victims have inefficient immune systems that fail to prevent complications when they suffer from infectious diseases or invasions of intestinal parasites.

A group of people who received the radiation dose of 150 rem (?)

---

14. Tsyb Commission 1989, p. 9.

showed signs of premature aging (10-12 years faster than normal rate).

Apparently the level of mortality and diseases in the Semipalatinsk region could be explained as remote consequences of atmospheric and above ground tests which were conducted there from 1949 through 1963 and *in 1965*.[15] In all probability, the medical consequences of underground nuclear tests are caused by seismic electromagnetic effects as well as leakage of radioactive gases into the atmosphere. A thorough medical and epidemiological study should be conducted to obtain final results.[16]

Some diseases may be attributable to the low socioeconomic status of the region relative to the rest of the Soviet Union. Test sites have generally been located in areas where people are relatively politically powerless and poorer. Thus, they have been more vulnerable to disease and have tended to receive less effective treatment when they do get sick, due to less-equipped health services. All these conditions confound any studies of radiation effects.

With only preliminary scientific results in hand, even the official commissions have echoed popular anger. There are also allegations that military personnel and the local population were used as guinea pigs. According to the report of the People's Deputies:

> The group of People's Deputies paid special attention to information that in the 50s the local population, and possibly military personnel, were used as experimental objects to study the effects of nuclear weapons testing.[17]

At the present time we have no details of the alleged experiments. We also have no data on doses to military personnel. Yet interviews in the Kazakh village of Karaul suggest that there was little attention to protecting the population. When the Soviet Union tested its first hydrogen bomb in 1953, Karaul was evacuated except for 40 people who were told to stay behind. "I witnessed the first H-bomb explosion,"

---

15. In January 1965 (after the Limited Test Ban Treaty) the Soviets conducted a nuclear explosion at the confluence of the Chagan and Ashisu Rivers for the principal purpose of creating a reservoir. The charge was detonated underground at a shallow depth and led to serious contamination of the surrounding area. For this reason, the People's Deputies Commission classified the explosion as "atmospheric."

16. Commission of People's Deputies 1990.

17. Commission of People's Deputies 1990.

said one inhabitant. "Afterward they gave us a check-up and the military men gave us some vodka as protection against radiation . . . No one ever told us that there was any danger." Another witness said, "Of the 40 people they left in this village, only six are alive today . . . The military men told us it is not dangerous at all." A third resident, who had lost five members of his immediate family to cancer, said, "For many years I believed that what our government was doing was necessary . . . We didn't know whether the atomic mushrooms were harmful or not."[18]

Novaya Zemlya

The two islands comprising Novaya Zemlya are located in a district of the Arkhangelsk region inhabited by the Nenetz people. The two islands together measure 923 kilometers in length and 81,300 square kilometers in area. They are 144 kilometers wide at the widest place and 32 kilometers wide at the narrowest. It is a cold and windy place, with a temperature ranging between -43° and +22.5° Celsius and an average of 242 days of snow cover per year. The testing area encompasses 90,200 square kilometers of land and sea.

The decision to use Novaya Zemlya as a nuclear weapons testing site was made in 1954. One reason was its isolation—the nearest village, Amderma, is 280 kilometers away. The much larger center of Arkhangelsk is 1,000 kilometers away, and three villages lie at intermediate distances. The 104 Nenetz families living on Novaya Zemlya were asked by the Soviet government to move to the mainland.

Air, surface, and underwater tests were conducted at Novaya Zemlya from 1957 until 1963, the year of the Limited Test Ban Treaty, after which testing was conducted underground.

Although available information is scarce, it does provide a hint about the problems associated with fallout from nuclear weapons testing. Table 12 shows the density of beta contamination at five locations in the Arkhangelsk region, as compared to Moscow and Alma Ata, the capital of Kazakhstan, as measured in 1962 and 1988.

---

18. Zheutlin 1990.

Table 12
BETA RADIATION LEVELS AT SOME LOCATIONS
IN THE SOVIET UNION (IN MILLICURIES/KM^2)

Location	Limits of variation of monthly averages 1962	1988	Maximum daily average 1962	1988
Archangelsk region				
Amderma	0.8-64.0	0.02-0.03	877.0	0.08
Dixon	0.8-13.0	0.03-0.08	208.0	0.24
Salehard	0.4-2.9	0.008-0.06	17.2	0.40
Naryan Mar	0.4-4.1	0.005-0.02	35.6	0.08
Anadyr	0.9-2.8	0.01-0.02	28.5	0.05
Moscow	1.4-5.7	0.04-0.09	26.6	0.34
Alma Ata	2.4-19.8	0.04-0.07	432.0	0.22

Source: Undated official document.

Environmental Effects of Underground Testing

The Soviet Union has conducted its 503 underground tests at many locations in its territory. As can be seen in Figure 6, most Soviet tests were underground. The multiple explosion sites mean that underground contamination potentially affects more territory and larger populations and constitutes a greater threat to future generations in the Soviet Union than in any other country.

The Tsyb Commission considered only the seismic impact of underground explosions. It did not discuss venting of radioactive materials from underground tests.

Tokhtarov presented some data regarding emissions from underground nuclear explosions. The first and perhaps largest release occurred in January 1965, from a nuclear explosion to excavate a water reservoir at the confluence of the Chagan and Ashisu rivers. His estimate of radiation levels "at traditional pastures and watering places" was 50 milliroentgens per hour, though the time after the explosion at which this level prevailed is not specified. The thyroid dose to children was estimated at 53 rems and the bone dose at 15 rems.[19]

Tokhtarov noted that prior to 1980 underground nuclear tests in the Soviet Union were conducted at shallow depths, and he implied that venting was the rule rather than the exception. According to the report, the military admits that about 30 percent of underground explosions at the test site (or about 100 tests) were followed by the release of radioactive gases. Also cited were three cases of venting in the late 1980s, despite the fact that these tests were conducted at depths of 500 to 600 meters:[20] on May 7, 1987, the radiation level in Semipalatinsk reached 350 to 500 microroentgens per hour; on September 18, 1987, the radiation level was 45 microroentgens per hour; and on February 13, 1989, the radiation level at the village of Chagan was 3,200 microroentgens per hour. (Typical natural background radiation is on the order of 10 microroentgens per hour.)

The Tsyb Commission did not discuss the long-term effects of the radioactive legacy that underground testing is leaving for future generations. This problem is in many ways even more serious in the Soviet Union than in the United States because of the large number of locations at which underground tests have been conducted. We have at present no data on environmental monitoring at these sites. Both the national and local commissions have urged a declassification of data.

Based on the coefficients that we have used for other countries and on approximate yields of the 503 Soviet underground tests, we arrive at decay-corrected estimates of the total amounts of three radionuclides being left behind by underground testing in the Soviet Union. These estimates are listed in Table 13.

In terms of weight, the plutonium-239 estimate is equivalent to 1,260 kilograms for all Soviet sites. This figure is consistent to within an order-of-magnitude with Balmukhanov's figure of about 500 kilograms of plutonium-239 at the Kazakhstan test site.[21]

In conclusion, the testing of nuclear weapons in the Soviet Union remains poorly understood. There were over 200 atmospheric tests and over 500 underground tests on Soviet territory. The available evidence

---

19. Tokhtarov 1990.
20. In the United States the depth criterion to prevent venting is: Depth = 400
   • (yield)0.333, where depth is in feet and yield in kilotons (U.S. Congress, Office of Technology Assessment 1989, p. 36).
21. Balmukhanov 1990.

Table 13
INVENTORIES OF SELECTED RADIONUCLIDES
DUE TO UNDERGROUND SOVIET TESTS
(DECAY-CORRECTED)

Radionuclide	Inventory
Strontium-90	2.3 million curies
Cesium-137	3.7 million curies
Plutonium-239	75,000 curies

points to the conclusion that protection of public health and the environment was scant, even compared to other nuclear weapons states. Environmental measurements of radiation, dosimetry, and tracking of exposed populations made public so far are inadequate to provide a good picture of population exposures. Medical data are insufficient to describe accurately cancer incidence or other measures of radiation effect.

Chapter 7

BRITISH TESTING IN AUSTRALIA

The United Kingdom tested nuclear weapons twelve times at three locations in Australia and nine times on Malden and Christmas Islands in the Pacific. The United States also conducted a 24-test series at Christmas Island. British staff participated in U.S. tests at Christmas Island in 1962. Since that time, Britain has tested its nuclear weapons at the Nevada Test Site in the United States.

We will consider the tests at Malden and Christmas Islands in Chapter 8.

Historical Context, Locations, Number, and Types of Tests

The location of the major test sites is shown in Figure 7. There were 12 atmospheric tests in all, carried out between 1952 and 1957, three at Monte Bello, two at Emu, and seven at Maralinga. They were air drop, tethered balloon, tower, and ground surface explosions. Both fission and activation products were formed, with immediate, heavy fallout coming to earth within a few hours and a few kilometers from the blast, as well as stratospheric injection via the fireball. Table 14 lists the

Figure 7

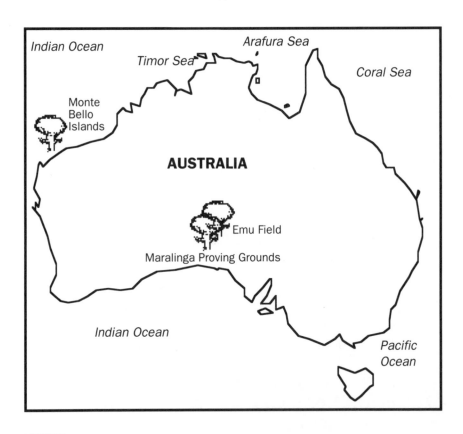

Atmospheric testing

Table 14
BRITISH TESTS IN AUSTRALIA

Location	Date	Yield	Remarks
Monte Bello	October 3, 1952	20 kilotons	
Emu Field	October 15, 1953	kiloton range	1953 tests yielded
Emu Field	October 27, 1953	kiloton range	40 kilotons total
Monte Bello	May 16, 1956	kiloton range	
Monte Bello	June 19, 1956	kiloton range	
Maralinga	September 27, 1956	kiloton range	1956 tests yielded
Maralinga	October 4, 1956	low yield	100 kilotons total
Maralinga	October 11, 1956	low yield	
Maralinga	October 22, 1956	kiloton range	
Maralinga	September 14, 1957	low yield	
Maralinga	September 25, 1957	kiloton range	
Maralinga	October 9, 1957	kiloton range	

Source: Defense Minister Killen, March 31, 1977, in Parliament.

nuclear tests conducted in Australia.

The British and French decisions to make or accelerate the development of their own nuclear weapons were spurred by the U.S. decision to keep its nuclear weapons secrets to itself and not collaborate on nuclear weapons with other countries. The U.S. prohibition on international collaboration was contained in a clause of the McMahon Act of 1946, which set up the U.S. Atomic Energy Commission to develop nuclear weapons. The British decision to build nuclear weapons independently meant a test site was needed.

The first test was conducted in Australia, which had been an independent commonwealth since 1901 but was still very much under British influence. On February 18, 1952, the Australian Prime Minister, Robert Gordon Menzies, made the following brief announcement:

> In the course of this year, the United Kingdom Government intends to test an atomic weapon produced in the United Kingdom. In close cooperation with the Government of the Commonwealth of Australia, the test will take place at a site in Australia. It will be conducted in conditions that will ensure that there will be no danger whatever from radioactivity to the health of the people or animals in the Commonwealth.[1]

The first British nuclear explosive was brought from Britain on the *HMS Plym* and detonated on the ship on October 3, 1952, near the Monte Bello Islands, off the northwest coast of Australia. One of the attractions of the Monte Bello site for the British nuclear establishment was that it resembled an estuary and thus would yield information about the effects of nuclear weapons on many of Britain's major cities, which are located on estuaries. The Australian Government had agreed to the test on the understanding that the British would have executive control. The Australians provided logistical support, but there was no technical collaboration. Three Australian scientists were present as observers only.

The need for a land test site had been recognized in 1950 and a place had already been selected. A long-range reconnaissance party from the rocket range at Woomera, in the South Australian desert, had found a section of desert scarred with clay pans, covered in red bush spinifex, mulga, and she-oak. The terrain contained large expanses of sand dune and drift, but in places was hard enough to allow landings of large

---

1. Tame and Robotham 1982. This serves as a general reference for the rest of the section.

transport planes. It was called Emu Field and was used for two explosions in 1953.

Logistical problems prompted the search for another site closer to the trans-continental railway line, and eventually Maralinga, about 80 kilometers north of the railway, was chosen. Maralinga, meaning "Field of Thunder" in the local Aboriginal language, was intended to be a more permanent test site. While it was being set up, two more explosions took place at Monte Bello in 1956. The first explosion at Maralinga occurred on September 27, 1956, the last on October 9, 1957. The temporary ban on atmospheric nuclear tests in the late 1950s reduced Maralinga's usefulness for major tests, but it was still used for what were called "minor trials."

Downwind Communities

Fallout Measurements

Fallout measurements on the Australian mainland following the first nuclear explosion in 1952 were very limited in scope and of dubious quality. A house roof some 500 miles from the test site was treated with a special paint and all run-off water was collected and filtered to collect suspended particulate matter. Similar filters were installed in Rockhampton, Cairns, and Brisbane on the east coast of Australia, and in Suva, Fiji. In Rockhampton the activity in the filter was 200 times background radiation, in Brisbane 10 times background. No radioactivity was found in filters from Cairns or Suva.[2]

Fallout measurements were also very limited after the October 1953 tests at Emu. There were persistent rumors that a "black mist" had rolled over a cattle station named Wallatinna, about 116 miles from ground zero. Both the white station manager's family and a group of Aborigines subsequently recalled the presence of something in the air "coming from the south, black, like smoke. I was thinking it might be a dust storm, but it was quiet, just moving . . . It was just rolling and moving quietly."[3]

By 1954, both scientists and the public in general were becoming

---

2. Royal Commission 1985, vol. 1, p. 117.
3. Yami Lester, an aboriginal resident at Wallatina, in evidence to the Royal Commission (Royal Commission 1985, vol. 1, pp. 174-175).

concerned about the hazards posed by atmospheric nuclear weapons tests. The fate of the crew of the Japanese boat *Lucky Dragon* had demonstrated the dangers all too clearly. So before the 1956 tests, the Australian Government formed two committees, the Maralinga Committee and the Maralinga Safety Committee. The Maralinga Committee's main job was to coordinate the Australian response to the needs of the U.K. team.

The safety committee operated for about one-and-a-half years and was reconstructed as the Atomic Weapons Test Safety Committee (AWTSC) with Professor (later Sir) Ernest Titterton as its Chair. The role of the Atomic Weapons Test Safety Committee was:

1. To examine information and other data supplied by the United Kingdom government relating to atomic weapons tests to be carried out from time to time in Australia. This examination was to determine whether proposed safety measures were adequate for the prevention of injury to persons or livestock and other property.
2. To advise the Australian Prime Minister, through the Minister of Supply, of the conclusions arrived at by the Committee as a result of such examination, and in particular of what alternative or more extensive safety measures were considered necessary or desirable.

Thus, although the Committee clearly had responsibility for the health of the Australian population, it had to exercise that responsibility based on information and other data supplied by the British government.

In actuality, it seemed that the role of the Atomic Weapons Test Safety Committee was mainly to reassure the Australian public that all was well. The newspapers at the time proclaimed the success of the tests and uncritically quoted the governmental press releases stating that there was no danger from fallout. But information known to the Committee and the government showed all too clearly that clouds of radioactive iodine released by the explosions had contaminated large areas of Australia.

By the time of the 1956 and 1957 tests, a more comprehensive program of fallout monitoring had been developed using both gummed film collectors and a more specialized program to monitor iodine-131. Following the two tests conducted at Monte Bello on May 16 and June 19, 1956, levels of contamination on the northwestern mainland exceeded 100 microcuries per square meter.[4] Fallout levels in high rainfall areas on the east coast reached ten microcuries per square meter four days after the tests.[5]

The specialized iodine-131 monitoring was carried out at the request of the British Agricultural Research Council, by Dr. Marston, the Division Chief in the Commonwealth Scientific and Industrial Research Organisation. The research program studied, among other things, the uptake of iodine-131 in the thyroids of cattle and sheep. For reasons of secrecy, Marston started his sampling program a few weeks before the first Maralinga test (September 27, 1956) and just after the 1956 Monte Bello tests (May, June). To his surprise, he found from the thyroids of animals he was testing that a band of radioactive fallout had passed over a relatively large area of northern Australia.[6] He had made his findings known to the Atomic Weapons Test Safety Committee, so was understandably surprised by the official statement that,

> We cannot over emphasize that the whole operation at Monte Bello was carried out without risk to life or property and absolutely no danger to the mainland.[7]

On July 4, 1956, Marston wrote to the Chief Executive Officer that,

> These [our thyroid findings] taken in conjunction with various "official" announcements in the press, can lead to one of two conclusions viz. either monitoring setup in use at present is incapable of doing what it aims to accomplish or someone is lying.[8]

Later, in October 1956, Marston found evidence that the October 11 test had delivered fallout onto Adelaide, the capital city of South Australia. Pressure was brought to bear on Marston and he was allowed to publish only edited versions of his results, Titterton (Chair of the Atomic Weapons Test Safety Committee) apparently having done the editing.

The four tests at Maralinga in 1956 produced complex patterns of fallout, which were detectable in all the major southeastern population

---

4. See maps in Royal Commission 1985, pp. 252 and 255. Butement et al. (1957) reported a maximum recorded fallout of 128 microcuries per square meter at Port Hedland in western Australia on June 19, 1956.
5. Butement et al. 1957.
6. Marston 1958.
7. Sir Arthur Fadden, June 21, 1956, in Parliament.
8. Milliken 1986, p. 297.

centers. Of the three 1957 tests, only the second one, on September 25, produced fallout greater than 10 microcuries per square meter. The activity from that test ranged between 10 and 100 microcuries per square meter and extended eastwards from the test site for a considerable distance.[9]

Dose Estimates and Health Effects

The evidence of health effects from radiation among Aboriginal populations is suggestive but somewhat inconclusive. The South Australian Health Commission assumed that the test areas were unused wasteland. However, groups of Aborigines often moved through the desert,[10] and Aborigines claimed that many of them became sick and even died. Before 1985 the British government admitted to only one incident of Aborigines in the heavily contaminated area, but ex-servicemen have stated that Aborigines were reported in prohibited areas on numerous occasions.[11]

Two South Australian Health Commission reports on the health effects of radiation on Aboriginal populations came out in the early 1980s, but these were inconclusive due to the inability to define precisely the population at risk, the lack of a control group, the unavailability of health records for the relevant period, and the doubtful accuracy of statistics such as birth records. One of these studies deemed it unlikely that standard epidemiological techniques could be applied successfully to demonstrate adverse long-term effects of radiation among Aborigines.[12]

In response to increasing pressure from veterans in the late 1970s, the government asked the Australian Ionising Radiation Advisory Committee (AIRAC) to investigate irradiation of test personnel and the effects on the Australian population of radioactive fallout. In the resulting study, published in 1983 and known as AIRAC 9, AIRAC claimed to have found no evidence that any Aborigines were injured by the nuclear tests.[13]

In 1984 the Royal Commission was established to investigate the British nuclear weapons tests in Australia. (The circumstances under

---

9. Royal Commission 1985, vol. 1, p. 364 (map); Dwyer et al. 1959.
10. Firth 1987, Chapter 7, p. 72.
11. Smith 1985, Chapter 1, pp. 25-27.
12. South Australian Health Commission 1981, 1983-1984.
13. Australian Ionising Radiation Advisory Council 1983.

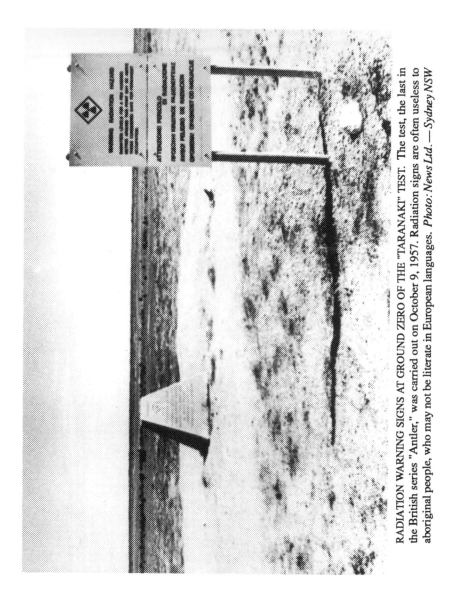

RADIATION WARNING SIGNS AT GROUND ZERO OF THE "TARANAKI" TEST. The test, the last in the British series "Antler," was carried out on October 9, 1957. Radiation signs are often useless to aboriginal people, who may not be literate in European languages. *Photo: News Ltd. — Sydney NSW*

which it was established are relevant to what information eventually came to light and when and are described in the next section.) The Royal Commission attempted to reconstruct dose profiles from the 1953 tests. The estimated maximum dose from both internal and external sources in the fallout area was 100 rems (to the intestine), with several people receiving up to 30 rems.

Overall, the Royal Commission drew several conclusions concerning downwind populations. On the one hand, their report said,

> because of the deficiencies in the available data, there is now little prospect of carrying out any worthwhile epidemiological study of those involved in the tests nor of others who might have been directly affected by them.[14]

At the same time, the Commission was critical of AIRAC and considered that at least some members of AIRAC did not approach their investigations with an open mind.[15] The Royal Commission concluded that it was probable that fallout from the major nuclear tests had caused cancers (that would not otherwise have occurred) in the Australian population.[16]

Armed Forces Personnel

Background to the Studies

During the testing periods, control of the site rested with the British authorities. Radiation safety was exercised by health physics teams from the U.K. Atomic Weapons Research Establishment at Aldermaston. An Australian health physics team was formed to work with the British team and three members went to the U.K. for specialized training. They in turn conducted training courses for the Australian teams. But for all the Australian involvement on the Maralinga site, the rules and regulations were British, and the U.K. team had the final responsibility for safety.

The way in which that responsibility was discharged came under increasingly close scrutiny, partly as a result of U.S. studies on health effects in their nuclear veterans, but mainly because of concern among

14. Royal Commission 1985, vol. 2, p. 609.
15. Royal Commission 1985, vol. 2, p. 596.
16. Royal Commission 1985, vol. 1, p. 102.

Australian nuclear veterans who noticed that large numbers of their former colleagues had contracted cancer.

In the late 1970s more and more veterans spoke out. This was not always easy because they often felt constrained by the very restrictive Official Secrets Act that they had signed during their period of military service. However, the pressure gradually increased. There were accounts of unpressurized aircraft flying through fallout clouds, decontamination of aircraft by personnel who were not wearing protective clothing, people requiring up to 15 showers to wash away the contamination, soldiers being sent into ground zero shortly after an explosion, lack of film badges, poor decontamination facilities, and men servicing vehicles not properly decontaminated.

As mentioned above, the government responded to the pressure by asking AIRAC to investigate. The 1983 report, AIRAC 9, downplayed the risks but did not allay the increasing concerns of the armed forces personnel. It has been criticized for relying only on the official version of events and failing to review any of the anecdotal evidence from the nuclear veterans.[17]

The change of federal government from Liberal to Labour in late 1982 had produced a different attitude toward the tests, which had all occurred when Liberal governments were in office. The Minister for Resources and Energy, Peter Walsh, announced that a scientific review of the available literature would be carried out. The review committee, known as the Kerr Committee, considered that there was sufficient strength to the veterans' case and sufficient doubts about the previous government's case, especially AIRAC 9, to warrant a detailed investigation. The Minister responded by establishing the Royal Commission, which produced its report in 1985.[18] Within the Australian legal system the Royal Commission has very important powers to subpoena witnesses, procure material evidence, and review any material within its terms of reference.

Major Studies

AIRAC was asked to look into the effectiveness of the measures taken to protect from injury Australians who assisted in the execution of the tests and to determine what effects, if any, there may have been

---

17. Robotham 1984, pp. 13-14.
18. Royal Commission 1985, vol. 1, vol. 2, and Conclusions and Recommendations.

on the health of the Australian population. AIRAC used radiation dosimetry information provided by the U.K. Atomic Weapons Research Establishment on Australians present at the nuclear tests and at experimental sites. Approximately 15,200 Australians were involved in the tests in some way, including many who were not directly involved in the tests and some who were not exposed to ionizing radiation. Approximately 1,300 were actually or potentially exposed to radiation through direct test involvement.

The Royal Commission acknowledged that much of the material published in AIRAC 9 was competently researched and capably considered, but there were important respects in which it was deficient, such as its failure to interview or seek out persons who might be able to assist with allegations of mismanagement, breaches of regulations, the black mist, or other alleged problems. The Royal Commission's final conclusions considered the report to be biased. Although a useful but limited radiological survey, AIRAC 9 was not described as objective and impartial.[19]

In the assessment of radiation doses and risks to the individual participants in the tests, it was pointed out by the Royal Commission that dose levels were not recorded for all participants. For example, the air and ground crews involved in the air sampling flights at the Hurricane and Totem 1 tests wore no film badges, nor were dosimeters carried in the aircraft. Thus, the dose estimates for individual participants in the tests are subject to varying degrees of uncertainty.[20]

Failure to provide radiation monitoring devices and instruction for air and ground crews was considered negligent. The Royal Australian Air Force should have been informed of the risks and provided with equipment to monitor the crews. In contrast, the evidence from servicemen aboard Royal Navy and Royal Australian Navy vessels disclosed no breaches of health and safety regulations nor excess radiation exposure to participants.[21]

Evidence of exposure of armed forces personnel to radiation came to light in the course of hearings related to compensation claims. The first claim for compensation was presented before the British High Court in November 1986, by British test participant Lance Corporal Melvyn Pearce, who suffered from lymphoma. He had served as an en-

---

19. Royal Commission 1985, Conclusions and Recommendations, pp. 29-30.
20. Royal Commission 1985, vol. 1, p. 99.
21. Royal Commission 1985, vol. 1, p. 136.

gineer on Christmas Island in 1957 and 1958. It was regarded as the test case for some 1,000 members of the British Nuclear Test Veterans Association, who claim to have developed cancer as a result of radiation exposure received during the 1950s British tests.[22]

The accounts given by the ex-servicemen revealed how groups of servicemen were made to march and crawl through radioactively contaminated areas. In the 1952 Hurricane test, men were still contaminated after an initial shower.[23] In other tests, officers stood in the open, two miles from ground zero, while some men were in trenches closer to the blast (the latter were the indoctrinated force who were there to get "real experience of nuclear war"[24]). Examples were repeatedly given of servicemen being within 10 miles of the detonation, and at the second Buffalo Test, they were less than two miles from detonation. An officer in a tank within two miles of the blast said the light was so bright one crew member saw the bones of his hands, "as though in an X ray." It was claimed that a group of six army officers were deliberately exposed to radiation in 1956 at the nuclear test range, and it had been decided the men should not wear protective clothing.[25]

The first recommendation of the Royal Commission's report was:

> The benefits of the compensations (Commonwealth Government Employees Act 1971), including the shifting of the onus of proof from the claimant to the Commonwealth, should be extended so as to include not only members of the armed forces who are at present covered by the Act, but also civilians who were at the test sites at the relevant times, and Aborigines and other civilians who may have been exposed to the black mist.[26]

The difficulty of establishing a link between radiation exposure and the onset of cancer has been demonstrated by the outcome of compensation claims for Australian nuclear veterans. By 1986, 204 claims had been lodged for illness or death, allegedly resulting from radiation exposure from the nuclear tests. Only six cases had been decided in favor of the veterans' claims.[27]

The Royal Commission came to the following conclusions on

---

22. May 1989.
23. Connor and Thomas 1985.
24. Milliken 1986, p. 162.
25. Hamer 1988.
26. Royal Commission 1985, Conclusions and Recommendations, p. 31.
27. Milliken 1986.

radiation doses and risks to test participants and the Australian public:

> By reason of the detonations of the major trials and the deposition of fallout across Australia, it is probable that cancers which would not otherwise have occurred have been caused in the Australian population. Their exposure to radiation as participants in the trial program has increased the risk of cancer among "nuclear veterans."[28]

Some estimates of the numbers of cancers involved are indicated by a follow-up of men who had been involved in the British Pacific tests. The study was initiated by a nationwide BBC television program in December 1982. The researchers invited first-hand accounts from participants and were given statistical data by the Department of Social Medicine at the University of Birmingham. Of approximately 13,000 men, 8,000 had a high incidence of leukemia and other reticulo-endothelial neoplasms. The number of deaths recorded was 27 compared to the expected 17.2. Of the 27 deaths, 16 were leukemias, nine lymphomas, one myeloma, and one polycythaemia vera. The researchers found 10 cases of cataract among those men under 25 years of age in 1958.[29]

The analysis in this report was based on numbers issued by the Prime Minister in February 1983—approximately 12,000 British servicemen, 1,500 British civilians, and 1,500 Australians. But after this study the government increased its estimate of test participants to 22,000. On the basis of these increased numbers, the authors of the report accepted that their results were no longer statistically significant, reflecting the problem of the dilution of high-risk groups that we discussed in Chapter 1.[30] They were nevertheless disturbed by the reported incidence of cataract, virtually unknown as a spontaneous occurrence in young men.[31]

The British Ministry of Defence believed that only a small proportion of those participating in the tests were exposed to ionizing radiation, and only to small doses. But because of the concern expressed by some veterans and the attendant publicity, the National Radiological Protection Board (NRPB) was commissioned to study the health of participants and investigate ill effects, if any, correlated with radiation exposure. From the Ministry of Defence archives, the NRPB obtained

28. Royal Commission 1985, vol. 1, p. 102.
29. Knox et al. 1983.
30. Connor 1988.
31. Boag et al. 1983.

information on the 22,347 men who participated in the British Nuclear Weapons Test Programs in Australia and the Pacific from 1952 to 1967. The men were followed up and compared for mortality and incidence of cancer with a 22,326 matched control group also obtained from the archives. There were 406 deaths from neoplasms in the participants and 434 in the controls, with 22 cases of leukemia and six cases of multiple myeloma in the participants as compared to six and zero, respectively, in the controls. These differences were statistically significant. However, although the mortality from leukemia and multiple myeloma in the participants was higher than would have been expected from national values, in the controls the incidence was substantially *lower* than expected, which makes it difficult to interpret the cause of the statistically significant difference. No relationship was found between cancer mortality and recorded doses of external radiation or type of test participation.

The study concluded that participation in the nuclear weapons test program did not have a detectable effect on the participants' life expectancy or on the overall risk of developing cancer, apart from the possible increased risk of developing multiple myeloma or leukemia other than chronic lymphatic leukemia. It further concluded that there was no evidence that participants who developed these diseases were exposed to unusual amounts of ionizing radiation.[32]

There are a number of problems with this study. Seventeen percent of test participants, mainly those from the Royal Air Force and Army, were not on the original list and were therefore excluded from the study. Some of the army personnel were not included in the study because their service records had been removed, as disability claims had been made. Radiation exposure data from personal dosimeters were available only for approximately 20 percent of participants.

One review of the study indicated that the increase in leukemia and multiple myeloma, significantly higher than the controls, must be of concern, as leukemia was the first cancer to appear in excess in Japanese A-bomb survivors and the rates of multiple myeloma rose after a latent period of only 15 years. The authors of that review concluded that some leukemias and probably multiple myelomas have resulted from radiation exposure during the tests.[33]

Another review of the same study pointed out that, although the ob-

32. Darby et al. 1988b.
33. Gardner 1988.

served difference in mortality from leukemia and multiple myeloma was mainly due to the extraordinarily low rates (compared to the national rates) for the diseases in the controls, still the mortality from the two cancers increased by 13 and 11 percent respectively in the participants.[34]

In addition, the rates were compared to findings for standardized mortality ratios for servicemen from the Decennial Supplements published by the Registrar General. The data suggested that by comparison the test participants had unusually high standardized mortality ratios for neoplasms of the reticuloendothelial system and the control group had unusually low values.[35] In response, the authors of the British (NRPB) report suggested that the difference in mortality from neoplasms of the reticuloendothelial system was principally due to an atypical low mortality in the controls.[36]

The findings of a study of New Zealand veterans who participated in the Christmas Islands tests (see Chapter 8) tend to reinforce the results of the British survey and suggest that the increase of leukemia among participants in these tests is a small but significant risk.

A weakness of this kind of epidemiological study is that the health effects in the high-risk groups have been diluted by mixing them with all the other personnel who participated in the tests. We have already discussed some examples of high-risk work. Some of those pertinent to the Australian situation are as follows:

1. About 400 people were involved in the post-test clean-up at Monte Bello after the first test in 1952. Of these, it is estimated that 31 received doses exceeding 3 roentgens, with the highest exposure being 5 roentgens.[37]
2. Aircraft crews in unpressurized planes (Lincoln bombers) spent up to 55 minutes in the fallout clouds following the 1953 tests. They probably received a higher dose than the crews of pressurized Canberra bombers, who received gamma doses of up to 21 roentgens.[38]

---

34. Hadlington 1988.
35. Sorahan 1988.
36. Darby and Doll 1988.
37. Royal Commission 1985, p. 125.
38. Royal Commission 1985, vol. 1, p. 207.

Isolation of the high-risk groups for separate study is likely to yield results which show much more definitive damage than the overall studies in which the entire group of test participants is matched against a control group. That some risk shows up even when the exposed population is diluted indicates that the smaller group of people engaged in high-risk activities faced a considerably larger risk.

Residual Environmental Contamination

The total amount of plutonium-239 dispersed as a result of the nine tests in the kiloton range in Australia would be about 1,350 curies, assuming 150 curies per test. Table 2, in Chapter 3, gives an estimate of the fission yield of the British tests in Australia until 1956 as about 160 kilotons. Assuming a total of about 200 kilotons for all tests in Australia (including the three in 1957), the amount of cesium-137 and strontium-90 dispersed would have been 32,000 and 20,000 curies respectively. About one-third of the cesium and strontium still remain in the atmosphere, on the ground, and in bodies of water.

At Monte Bello there is no acute radiation hazard from the tests conducted there.

Radiation levels at Emu exceed the levels set for continuous occupation; however, the area is inhospitable for other reasons and unlikely to become a permanent campsite.

At Maralinga, there continue to be a number of radiological and toxic hazards: plutonium-239 fragments and contamination at four "minor test" sites, plutonium-239 buried in pits, uranium at several sites, beryllium at five sites, and residual radiation at some of the ground zeros. The major hazard is from the plutonium-239 which was scattered on and near the site during the minor trials. The Royal Commission estimated that there could be between 25,000 and 50,000 plutonium-contaminated fragments, with a total plutonium-239 content of 32 curies.[39] One plutonium-239 contamination plume extended 12 miles from the test pad. This is in addition to the atmospheric dispersal from the major tests discussed above.

The Royal Commission recommended that the Maralinga range be cleaned up and that the cost be borne by the British government. A joint Australian/British Task Force has been established to assess this

---

39. Royal Commission 1985, vol. 2, p. 550.

problem.

The Australian Radiation Laboratory has continued to study the plutonium-239 contamination of Maralinga,[40] contributing to a report by the Technical Assessment Group presented before the Australian Parliament on November 14, 1990.[41] This study gave final estimates on the contamination of the test area and of the costs of clean-up. It showed that an extensive clean-up would cost more than $650 million, which would give Aborigines unrestricted access to their land and enable them to pursue their traditional ways of life. The report also presented other options, which cost less and would allow unrestricted access to up to 90 percent of the area.

---

40. Australian Radiation Laboratory 1986, 1988, 1989, and 1990.
41. Technical Assessment Group 1990.

Chapter 8

BRITISH AND U.S. TESTING AT CHRISTMAS ISLAND

Historical Context, Locations, Number, and Types of Tests

British military planners considered test sites worldwide before settling on Australia. Eight places in the Indian Ocean and four in the Atlantic Ocean were rejected because they were too populated or conditions were thought unsuitable. The "Pacific Islands" were rejected because they were even further in time from the U.K. than Australia, they were "relatively densely populated," and air access was difficult.

Australia's unquestioning acceptance of British atmospheric nuclear tests waned in 1956, and mounting public concern over reports that Australia had been "top-dressed" with fallout ruled out testing the British hydrogen bomb on that continent. Britain looked to more isolated regions. With impending test ban treaties, Britain was determined to test the hydrogen bomb before it was too late. So it overcame its previous qualms about the Pacific Islands and settled upon Christmas Island, at the equator midway between Tahiti and Hawaii (see Figure 8).

In land area it is the largest coral atoll in the Pacific, and now part of far-flung Kiribati, previously the Gilbert and Ellice Islands. Inhabited for 3,000 years, it was "discovered" by Captain James Cook on Christmas Day of 1777.

Squadron Leader Roland Duck described the selection criteria in a BBC documentary: "When we were first given the task of finding a site, we decided the nicest way and the easiest way was to find a vast expanse of water. The largest amount of water with the least land is the Pacific. So we took a large map of the Pacific and we really settled our finger and put it down rather like picking a winner and we got Christmas Island and Malden Island".[1]

It was a sad day for the "winner." This was to be the site of seven hydrogen bomb and two fission bomb explosions and a subsequent U.S. test series. Despite the diplomatic protests of Japan and India, Britain's first H-bomb exploded on May 15, 1957. The first series, Grapple 1 - 3, were high air burst H-bombs off uninhabited Malden Island, 600 kilometers to the south of Christmas Island. The second series, Grapple x - Z4, involved four more ocean air-bursts and two smaller atomic bombs balloon-suspended at 450 meters over the end of Christmas Island. Most of these tests were in the megaton range. By 1958 the major British tests were completed. Smaller trials continued until 1963.

The U.S. testing program at Christmas Island, undertaken after the collapse of the East-West moratorium of the late 1950s, consisted of Operation Dominic, a series of 24 "shots" between April and July 1962. Three hundred U.K. servicemen and 3,200 from the United States were involved. In return for the United States use of the base, the British negotiated access to the American data.

The island was vacated in 1964, and survey and clean-up operations continued until 1967.

Downwind Communities

Christmas Islanders

Christmas Island rises to a maximum of three meters above sea level. Unreliable rainfall and poor growing conditions in the coral "soil" had kept habitation to around 300 Micronesians. These included in-

---

1. British Broadcasting Corporation 1983.

Figure 8

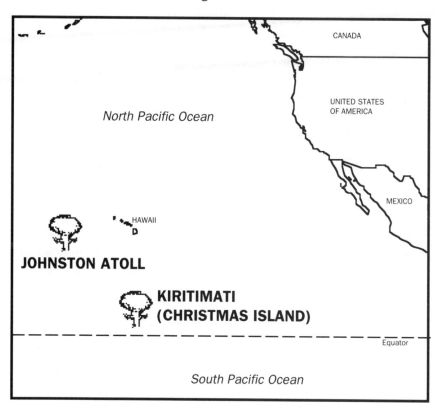

LEGEND

Atmospheric testing

digenous inhabitants as well as single men and families from others of
the Gilbert and Ellice Islands, who usually stayed for two or three years,
providing cheap labor for copra production. Malden Island was, and
remains, uninhabited.

Assured by the safety of the three hydrogen bomb tests off Malden
Island, the British government transferred the program to Christmas Island itself. Families were taken to off-shore boats for each hydrogen
bomb test. The "smaller" atomic bombs were exploded off the far end
of Christmas Island. Micronesians remained on land for these and were
asked to protect their eyes from the flash, and to leave doors and shut-
ters open to reduce damage from blast.

During the U.S. tests, evacuation was thought unnecessary.
However, two large explosions caused upset, and many of the
Micronesians chose to leave the island for subsequent tests. Those who
stayed witnessed the "fire in the sky." Canned food was provided for
three months after the U.S. tests. Micronesians were advised to avoid
coconuts and fish during this time.

There are anecdotal reports of eye problems and increased miscarriage. Probably less than 25 percent of those present for the tests remain
on Christmas Island, the others having scattered through the Central
Pacific. The Kiribati government has asked the United Kingdom for an
independent health study and compensation.

Tongareva Islanders

Tongareva, or Penrhyn Island, of the Cook Island group, lies 550
kilometers to the south of Malden Island. A weather station was established there. The atmospheric effects of some explosions were seen
from Tongareva. There are reports of ciguatera at the time of the tests
(reefs were blasted for shipping access), and a local concern persists
about cancer deaths on the island.[2]

Armed Forces Personnel

During the 1957 tests the New Zealand frigates Pukaki and Rotoiti
monitored the weather and the Royal Air Force Shackletons patrolled
large expanses of ocean to keep out "unauthorized" shipping. A fleet of

---

2. Mr. Wilkie Rasmussen, formerly of Tongareva, in conversation with Dr.
Graham Gulbransen, Rarotonga, 1985.

British warships and the two New Zealand frigates, with about 2,000 men in all, were stationed 40 kilometers from ground zero. Seamen not essential to running the ships were on deck wearing "anti-flash" gear: cotton overalls with hoods and dark goggles. These outfits were thought unnecessary and not worn for the later tests. To avoid the flash they were instructed to face away from the explosion for the first five seconds. Pre-wetting was carried out: the ships were hosed down prior to the detonations for easy decontamination. However, official reports say there was no contamination.[3]

Other military personnel and civilians were assembled on different parts of Christmas Island to watch the tests, some 40 kilometers from ground zero. Thirty-nine men from the Fiji Royal Navy Volunteer Reserve and up to 60 other Fiji servicemen attended the tests. Their former leader, Ratu Inoke Bainimarama, said the men had been given name tags and numbers to hang from their necks in case they were killed during the explosion. Scientists and officers were in a special bunker 15 to 20 kilometers from ground zero. The procedure remained the same for most tests.

Canberra "sniffer" aircraft were flown through the cloud just minutes after the explosion, collecting samples. An Air Ministry document of 1957 seems to downplay the danger of contamination:

> With a true air burst (i.e. where the fireball does not touch the ground) the up-draught caused by the rapidly rising mushroom cloud may be sufficient to draw upwards a stream of dust and debris from the ground. This stream rises upward towards the center of the toroid or smoke ring of the main cloud and appears to join the main cloud and so form the stem of the mushroom. In fact, the stream of dust particles and debris pass through the center of the toroid and curl round down the outside but do not mix with the main cloud. Any radioactivity originally induced in the dust and debris of this stream is not significantly increased nor do the particles act as centers on which the unfissioned or vaporized weapons materials or the fission products condense. When this dust and debris falls out there is relatively little residual radiation from it. The original weapon material and fission products in the toroid which have already condensed into much smaller particles, will rise much higher, take longer to fall, be much more widely spread and decay more before reaching the ground, so that they too, cause little residual radioactivity.[4]

---

3. McEwan 1988.
4. United Kingdom Air Ministry 1957, p. 142.

Further:

> If evidence points to a burst of this type there should be no need for the whole radiological defence organization to go into action.[5]

However there was acknowledgement of the risk of rainout:

> Residual radiation is of no military significance from a high or medium air burst except in the case of a low yield weapon (less than 10 [kilotons]) burst in rain, when rain-out may be a hazard.[6]

It appears that Malden Island was contaminated by induced radioactivity. Following Grapple 2, two men (without film badge or Geiger counter) spent two days retrieving monitoring instruments from ground zero. The instruments showed high readings: 3.80 and 4.20 roentgens. One man developed generalized blistering and was evacuated.[7]

The Canberra crews' mission was to fly through the densest part of the cloud and take samples. They were volunteers who knowingly placed themselves at risk of high radiation exposure, with a mean dose of 50.5 millisieverts per man per test.[8] On landing, clothing was discarded, and men were washed, scrubbed, and sometimes shaved. One pilot was sent home and required to have blood tests for a year. Royal Air Force aircraft were known to have flown inadvertently through the fallout cloud.[9] Those decontaminating the aircraft by hosing and scrubbing with sea water were identified by the Ministry of Defence as "liable to have been exposed to radiation."[10] Although they wore respirators, their cotton protective clothing was often soaked through.[11]

On the observer ships, "the use of protective clothing declined, or even ceased, with the latter tests in the series, apparently because it was considered that no significant radiation exposure was occurring."[12]

The researchers commissioned by the BBC television program to survey the British nuclear veterans (the study mentioned in Chapter 7) noted "an abnormally high incidence of leukemia and other reticuloen-

---

5. United Kingdom Air Ministry 1957, p. 148.
6. United Kingdom Air Ministry 1957, p. 129.
7. Blakeway and Lloyd-Roberts 1985, p. 157.
8. Darby et al. 1988a.
9. Blakeway and Lloyd-Roberts 1985, pp. 168-169.
10. Darby et al. 1988a.
11. British Broadcasting Corporation 1983.
12. Pearce et al. 1990, p. 6.

UNDERWATER NUCLEAR BLAST IN UNITED STATES' OPERATION DOMINIC, CHRISTMAS ISLAND, MAY 11, 1962. The destroyer USS Agerholm is in the foreground. *Photo: U.S. Navy, by D.D. Mann*

dothelial system neoplasms" in servicemen at Christmas Island.[13]

A study published by the Wellington School of Medicine on New Zealand veterans of Pacific tests examined data for 528 men who participated in the Christmas Island and Malden Island tests.[14] (There may have been up to 600 on the two frigates.) The control group consisted of 1,504 men who were in the Royal New Zealand Navy during the same period (1957-58) but were not involved in the tests. Both groups were identified from Ministry of Defence records and through the media.

Mortality and cancer deaths were studied. The death rate in the two groups was similar: 13 percent of the test veterans and 12 percent of the controls had died from 1957 to 1987, hence a relative risk of about 1.1. The rates for most causes of death were also very similar. The relative risk for causes other than cancer was 0.96, and for cancers was 1.38. If the hematologic cancers are taken out, the remaining cancers hold a risk of 1.14, or roughly the expected number. There were seven deaths from hematologic cancer in the test veterans (a relative risk of 3.3), including four leukemias (relative risk, 5.6). The authors concluded that although the numbers were small, the findings for leukemia were similar to those of the National Radiological Protection Board study of British participants in the nuclear weapons tests and suggest that there is some increased risk of leukemia among test participants.[15]

Of 194 Royal Navy personnel who were considered to have had significant radiation exposure, data suggest an exposure of 5.2 millisieverts per man, although data derived from the film badges of New Zealand naval veterans is not available. The New Zealanders attended 3.6 tests per man on average, compared to about 1.2 tests for the British test participants. Thus, exposure could have been higher in the New Zealand group, although there is no reason to believe the Royal New Zealand Navy duties involved more exposure per test. Finally, there are no data on internal radiation exposure.[16]

Dr. A.C. McEwan of the National Radiation Laboratory in Christchurch, New Zealand, on the other hand, claims that "significant intake of fallout radionuclides would not be likely without accompanying external radiation exposure." He concludes that "the distribution of

---

13. Knox et al. 1983.
14. Pearce et al. 1990.
15. Pearce et al. 1990.
16. Pearce et al. 1990, p. 6.

cancers in the test participants is well within the range of values which could be expected by chance. Further, the study does not provide evidence of exposure to radiation."[17]

The Air Ministry document of 1957 seems to support Dr. McEwan's thinking:

> The internal hazard from residual radiation is not an important factor in current military operations since it produces body damage slowly over a long period of time. Before it becomes dangerous to health the radioactive matter must enter the bloodstream, from which it can be deposited in the bones, liver and other vital organs. Radioactive material which does not get into the bloodstream is evacuated by the normal functions of the body.[18]

Unfortunately neither the NRPB nor the Wellington report detailed the amount of fallout anticipated or measured. Moreover, in this case, as in the others we have cited, the high risk groups from among the test participants were not studied separately. The possibility of significant internal doses to a small group of people due to the nature of the work and/or locations must be examined very carefully, based on the descriptions of the participants themselves.

The Ministry of Defence has agreed to the recommendation that a follow-up study be done in five years. War pensions are to be paid to veterans and widows for hematologic cancers.

Environmental Contamination

Further grounds for concern were exposed in *Just Testing,* by journalist Derek Robinson.[19] His interviews with Professor Joseph Rotblat, London University nuclear physicist and recipient of the IPPNW Distinguished Citizen Award, suggest that stratospheric condensation fell as radioactive rain, like the black rain of Hiroshima and Nagasaki. According to Joseph Rotblat's hypothesis, there could have been self-induced rainout at Christmas Island, which means that each explosion might have caused some rainout. These rainouts might have washed

---

17. McEwan 1990.
18. United Kingdom Air Ministry 1957, p. 148H.
19. Robinson 1985, p. 142.

radioactive particles from land to sea where some of this radioactivity would have become concentrated as it passed through the food chain.

The total amount of plutonium-239 dispersed as a result of the nine British and 24 U.S. tests and over Christmas Island would be about 4,950 curies, assuming 150 curies per test. Table 2, in Chapter 3, gives an estimate of the fission yield of the British tests at Christmas Island of about 10 megatons. On this basis, the amount of cesium-137 and strontium-90 dispersed would have been 160,000 and 100,000 curies respectively. About one-third of the cesium and strontium still remain in the atmosphere, on the ground, and in bodies of water. We do not have a separate estimate of the fission yields of the 24 U.S. tests at Christmas Island, therefore the total fission products still remaining from tests at Christmas Island is larger.

Chapter 9

FRENCH TESTING

Locations, Number, and Types of Tests

The first French nuclear tests were conducted in Algeria between 1960 and 1965. The first test took place at Reggan on February 13, 1960, when Algeria was still a colony in the throes of a war for independence. In all, 14 nuclear weapons tests were conducted at the two Algerian locations shown in Figure 9, four atmospheric and 10 underground. The French government made preparations to move the testing to its colony Polynesia after Algeria won its independence.

The French test sites in the Pacific are Moruroa and Fangataufa, two atolls in the southeastern area of the Tuamotu Archipelago, French Polynesia (see Figure 10). The Moruroa Atoll ($21.83°$ Southern latitude and $138.88°$ Western longitude) is one of the largest coral atolls in that area. The atoll, in the form of an incomplete ring encircling a lagoon, measures 26 kilometers east to west and 10 kilometers north to south. The 65-kilometer-long reef-crown, with a mean height of two meters and rarely exceeding 400 meters in width, is open, leaving a 5-kilometer-wide passage into the lagoon on the northwestern side. The lagoon has an average depth of 40 meters and is the crater of an extinct underwater volcano, around which outer coral has pushed up above sea

Figure 9

LEGEND

 Atmospheric testing

 Underground testing

level to form the visible rim. The distance to the nearest inhabited island (Tureia) is 100 kilometers, the distance to Tahiti is 1,200 kilometers, and New Zealand is 4,200 kilometers away. The atoll was uninhabited before the installation of the test center.[1]

Fangataufa, a much smaller atoll, is located 41 kilometers south-southeast of Moruroa (22.25° Southern latitude and 138.63° Western longitude). It measures five by eight kilometers and was also uninhabited before the tests. In contrast to Moruroa, Fangataufa was a closed atoll. The French military therefore opened a 400-meter gap in the coral ring to enable ships to enter the lagoon.[2]

From 1966 to 1990, 167 nuclear test explosions occurred on these two atolls. These tests were used for the development of at least eight types of nuclear warheads.

Of the 167 tests, 44 were atmospheric, 39 over Moruroa, five over Fangataufa. The overall yield of these atmospheric explosions was 12,000 kilotons of TNT. The first atmospheric test was performed on Moruroa on July 2, 1966, the last on September 15, 1974. Most of the early tests were performed on the surface or on a barge anchored in the lagoon. Because of the large amount of radioactive fallout resulting from the low-altitude bursts, most further tests were performed with warheads hanging under balloons. Very few tests were conducted as airdrops from planes. One test, designed to check the security apparatus of the warhead, resulted in no nuclear detonation, but the fragmented bomb spread plutonium-239 over the coral rim. The first explosion of a two-stage fission-fusion device on August 24, 1968, at Fangataufa, was the largest explosion, with a yield of 2.6 megatons.

After June 5, 1975, the tests were conducted underground. Since then, four to 11 underground explosions have been conducted each year. Of the total, three were in Fangataufa in 1975 and 1988, the other 120 at Moruroa. The yields of these explosions have never been released officially, but the total yield is estimated at about 2,500 kilotons of TNT. This estimate is based largely upon observations by the New Zealand Department of Scientific and Industrial Research and the Swedish National Defense Research Institute, which recorded and analyzed the seismic data from these tests.[3]

The underground tests have been conducted at the bottom of shafts bored 500-1,200 meters into the basalt core of the atoll. Initially these

---

1. Atkinson et al. 1984, Cousteau Foundation 1988, and Burrows et al. 1989.
2. Atkinson et al. 1984, Cousteau Foundation 1988, and Burrows et al. 1989.
3. Swedish National Defense Research Institute 1987 and Smith 1989.

Figure 10

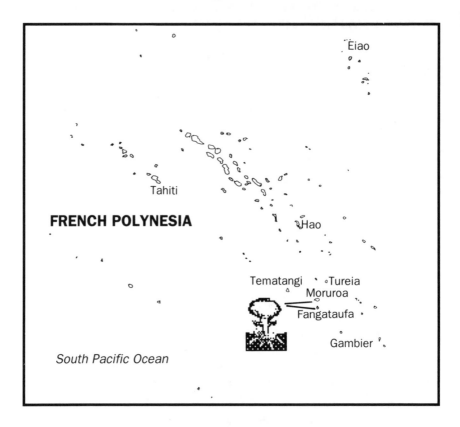

Atmospheric and underground testing

shafts were drilled in the outer rim of the atoll. In 1981, most likely due to the weakening of that rim, the tests with higher yields were shifted to shafts drilled under the lagoon itself. In 1986 all tests were shifted to this so-called *zone central.*[4]

Historical Context of Testing

The independence of Algeria in 1962 threatened further testing at the Algerian sites. The French Ministry of Defense therefore started to look for other suitable test sites. Possible locations included Clipperton Island in the Pacific as well as the Kerguelen Islands in the Southern Indian Ocean, which were eventually ruled out because of their hostile climate and remote location. The final decision was in favor of the uninhabited islands of Moruroa and Fangataufa, and in 1964 the "Centre d'-Experimentation du Pacifique" (CEP) was constructed.[5]

The main argument favoring the selection was that only 5,000 inhabitants lived within a 1,000-kilometer radius of the planned ground zero in Moruroa and that it would therefore be suitable for atmospheric testing. Although the 1963 Limited Test Ban Treaty banned the testing of nuclear weapons in the atmosphere, underwater, and in space, France was not a signatory to it, and the French government under President de Gaulle announced that it would continue its atmospheric nuclear tests using the Moruroa Atoll. (According to U.S. government sources, President Kennedy offered help in the development of a French nuclear program if France would stop atmospheric testing. This offer was refused by the French government.)[6]

In 1972 the French government bowed to public pressure from Pacific and Latin American countries. The government tried to find an appropriate location for underground testing. The island initially considered, Eiao, in the Marquesas Group, was found to be unsuitable because of fragile basalt layers. In 1973 Fangataufa was chosen, and in 1974 President Giscard d'Estaing announced that as of that year only underground tests would be performed. After initial tests in Fangataufa, the testing was moved back to Moruroa, presumably to avoid the costs of running two test sites.[7] However, after many tests, Moruroa was

---

4. Burrows et al. 1989 and May 1989.
5. Direction des Centres d'Expérimentations Nucléaires 1985.
6. Greenpeace New Zealand 1985, Hughes 1988, Burrows et al. 1989.
7. Danielsson 1984.

deemed too fragile for larger underground testing, and in 1988 a high-ranking French officer commented that certain larger tests would be relocated to Fangataufa to avoid serious damage to the rock of Moruroa. Although the remark was later denied, on November 13, 1988, another test was performed at Fangataufa.[8]

Sources of reliable information on the tests and their outcome are limited due to the extreme secrecy of the French military. Limited investigations by four groups have been permitted by the French authorities in recent years: a French scientific mission in 1982;[9] a New Zealand, Australian, and Papua New Guinea scientific mission in 1983;[10] the Cousteau scientific mission in 1987;[11] and the mission of the Association of French Physicians for the Prevention of Nuclear War (AMFPGN), the IPPNW affiliate, in 1990.[12]

The reports of these expeditions are the most important available source of information on the consequences of the testing. All these missions were extremely restricted in duration—three to five days—and in preparation time. They were, therefore, only exploratory. All four missions were restricted in their access to relevant data, sites, or samples, such as coral and sediment from within the lagoon and specific areas of the atoll. Epidemiological data presented by French authorities were insufficient or unreliable. Despite these deficiencies, these studies as well as New Zealand and Swedish seismic data did produce significant insights, and are, to date, the best sources of information on the effects of French testing.

Downwind Communities

The French government has not made public any documents about nuclear tests in Algeria. In the absence of official documentation about armed forces participation, participation of Algerians, and dose and contamination levels, there has been mostly speculation and rumor about all of these subjects. The one figure that we have seen on radiation doses was reported by Greenpeace:

---

8. Burrows et al. 1989.

9. Tazieff 1982.

10. Atkinson et al. 1984.

11. Cousteau Foundation 1988.

12. Association des Médecins Français pour la Prévention de la Guerre Nucléaire 1990.

The first underground test, on 1 May 1962, code-named Beryl, was to test the prototype for the AN 11 bomb for the Mirage IVA aircraft. Despite adverse winds, and against the advice of the Commission of Nuclear Safety the explosion went ahead because two VIPs, one from the Ministère des Armées, were present. Twelve soldiers were contaminated when radioactive vapor escaped through a fissure in the rock; nine of them received more than 100 rem of radiation.[13]

Moruroa was selected for atmospheric testing because only 5,000 inhabitants lived within a 1,000-kilometer radius of the testing site. Yet, the initial danger-zone around the test site, which was to be kept free of planes and ships during a test, contained seven inhabited atolls. When this was pointed out to the French authorities, they reduced the radius of the zone designated as dangerous, but the atoll of Tureia, with about 60 inhabitants, 100 kilometers away from Moruroa, remained in the danger area. This island seems to have received severe radioactive fallout several times. One occasion was the test series of June and July 1967, when two French meteorologists on Tureia were evacuated two days after a test and transferred to the hospital at Hao. A complete evacuation of Tureia took place in 1968.[14] Despite these evacuations, the French authorities described the radiation doses on Tureia and Gambier from these 1967 and 1968 tests as not more than 75 millirems per year.[15]

The French Atomic Energy Commission acknowledged many years later that the 1966 Aldebarran tests covered the islands of Mureia, Tamoure, and Gambier with radioactive fallout resulting in radiation doses of 200 to 400 millirems.[16]

Because the immediate downwind communities are very small and under the control of the French government and independent radiation data are not available, the impact of the atmospheric tests on nearby communities cannot be judged. French military control over the health system of Polynesia is an obstacle to data collection. Health statistics from the period of atmospheric testing were either not collected, poorly collected, or not published. Missions of longer duration, a lifting of the "military-secret" classification on health and environmental aspects of testing, and careful epidemiological surveys would be needed to as-

---

13. May 1989, p. 132.
14. Hughes 1988.
15. French Atomic Energy Commission 1988.
16. French Atomic Energy Commission 1988.

FRENCH TEST IN POLYNESIA.   *Photo: United Nations, by Sygma*

sess the radiological impact of testing on the health of the population of the region.

The most intense monitoring of the Pacific region was performed by the National Radiation Laboratory of the New Zealand Department of Health, in cooperation with the Meteorological Service, the Australian Radiation Laboratory, and the governments of various Pacific islands. These measurements show that, although fission products from the tests were expected to circle the globe in an eastward direction, reaching the southern Pacific again after three weeks, rapid increases in radioactivity concentration in the days immediately after a test were occasionally observed in various Southern Pacific monitoring stations, indicating that radioactive material had been caught up and swept west to the central South Pacific.

The whole South Pacific region could be considered a downwind community. Total beta activity in the air was elevated for all monitoring stations in New Zealand as well as on Pacific islands including Fiji, Samoa, Tonga, and Tahiti for the whole period from 1966 to 1975. The same is true for total beta activity in rain. Measurements of gamma emitters in air at Tahiti returned to pre-test levels in 1975, after being elevated for the five previous years. Approximate mean effective dose equivalent commitments from nuclear test fallout in New Zealand, Fiji, and Tahiti returned to pre-test levels finally between 1975 and 1980.[17] All these data suggest a strong linkage between the concentration of fission products and French atmospheric tests from 1966 until 1974.

In a broader sense, downwind communities also include the South American countries. Most tests were performed with winds blowing to the east to avoid direct contamination of the Pacific islands west of Moruroa. Radiation levels of up to 12 millirems were attributed to the French tests in areas as far away as Peru and Baja California.[18]

Armed Forces Personnel

The tests at Moruroa have been shrouded in extreme secrecy. All exposure information is controlled by the French military and nuclear establishment. Measurements of radiation exposure of armed forces personnel have never been made available to scientists or the public. No known follow-up of exposed personnel of the sort done on British,

17. Atkinson et al. 1984.
18. French Atomic Energy Commission 1988.

Australian, and New Zealand personnel involved in British tests has taken place. Nevertheless, it is reasonable to assume that comparable exposures may have occurred. Measurements were performed by airplanes and helicopters flying into the radioactive clouds. There are also reports of equipment, planes, ships, and shelters needing to be decontaminated after certain tests.[19]

To estimate the number of potentially exposed personnel, it is relevant to consider the organizational structure of the CEP. The Center is run by the government authority "Direction des Centres d'-Experiméntations Nucléaires" (DIRCEN), under the control of the French Ministry of Defense. This authority has personnel on the atoll of Moruroa and small peripheral stations on the atolls of Tureia, Tematangi, and Reao. Between 3,000 and 3,600 people, military and civilian, are based at these locations. In the early 1960s the atoll of Hao was used as a rear base for assembling the nuclear weapons to be tested, which came from France by plane. This air-base, 400 kilometers northwest of Moruroa, houses about 400 people, of whom 270 are French military personnel. An additional 1,100 people are based in Tahiti, providing administrative and back-up services for the testing center.[20]

The first and only report about problems encountered by personnel at the CEP came from the civilian technicians and engineers employed to conduct tests on the atoll. A report by their trade union released in 1981 gave detailed information on the careless way in which waste has been managed on Moruroa Atoll. The report does not contain radiation measurements.[21]

In summary, it seems highly likely that French and Polynesian civilian and military personnel at the CEP were exposed to radiation from the tests. However, the health implications of this exposure cannot be stated with any precision, due to lack of published radiation exposure data, epidemiological studies, or reasonable follow-up.

Hot Spots

At least two hot spots in the South Pacific have been identified by radiation measurements. Both are linked to rainouts. One occurred in

19. Danielsson 1984.
20. Burrows et al. 1989 and Direction des Centres d'Expérimentations Nucléaires 1985.
21. Conféderation Française Démocratique du Travail 1981.

Samoa, 3,610 kilometers from Moruroa, on September 12, 1966. This was a consequence of test Betelgeuse on the previous day, in which a 120-kiloton bomb hanging under a balloon was exploded at a height of 600 meters, despite worsening wind conditions. (President de Gaulle attended this test, and it has been suggested that this was why the bomb was detonated despite unfavorable winds.[22]) As a result of a rainout, the total beta activity in rain in Apia/Samoa in the year 1966 increased from a normal level of around 200 megabecquerels per square kilometer to 370,000 megabecquerels per square kilometer.

Another incident of similar magnitude occurred at Tahiti on July 19, 1974, following a test on July 17th or 18th of unknown yield and burst height. As a consequence, the average concentration of total beta activity in the air, which is normally below 0.3 millibecquerels per cubic meter, increased to 1,460 millibecquerels per cubic meter in Papeete, Tahiti. The effective dose equivalent from nuclear test fallout due to external short-lived gamma exposure increased from below one millisievert to 154 millisieverts.[23] It is not known whether there have been additional incidents because detailed information for other locations in French Polynesia is not available.

Environmental Effects of Atmospheric Testing

The total amount of plutonium-239 dispersed as a result of the 45 announced French atmospheric tests, including the four in Algeria, would be about 6,750 curies, assuming 150 curies per test. Table 2, in Chapter 3, gives an estimate for the fission yield of the announced French atmospheric tests of about 10.9 megatons. On this basis, the amount of cesium-137 and strontium-90 dispersed would have been 1.7 million curies and 1.1 million curies respectively. About one-half of the cesium and strontium still remain in the atmosphere, on the ground, and in water bodies. French testing in the Pacific was the source of almost all the atmospheric fission product contamination, due to the much larger number of tests and the far greater yields of the French tests there than in Algeria.

---

22. Burrows et al. 1989.
23. Atkinson et al. 1984.

Environmental Effects of Underground Testing at Moruroa

The possible environmental effects of underground testing include short-term and long-term effects. At the time of the explosion, fracturing of the atoll surface can trigger landslides, tsunamis (tidal waves), and earthquakes. There is also evidence that radionuclides have vented to the environment. Possible long-term effects include leakage of fission products to the biosphere and transfer of dissolved plutonium-239 from the lagoon to the ocean and the food chain.

Physical Damage to the Reef

The upper layer of the atoll is made up of reef carbonates, mainly limestone. This limestone cover is approximately 300 meters thick in the south of the atoll, increasing to 430 to 550 meters in the north. The upper part of this limestone layer is undolomitized and comprises porous coral debris, approximately 125 meters thick. The lower part is dolomitized and therefore quite compact.

The limestone layer is separated from the underlying volcanic material by a transitional zone of variable thickness, composed mainly of weathered clays. It can vary in thickness from 40 to 45 meters below the atoll to a mere 50 centimeters or even nothing beneath most of the lagoon. The clay zone is impervious. The underlying volcanics are initially aerial volcanics, which then change to more homogeneous submarine volcanics at greater depths.

Each scientific mission to Moruroa has described severe damage to the integrity of at least the carbonate part of the atoll. The damage includes fissures in the limestone and surface subsidences of large areas of the atoll. Fissures are propagated by the testing, a result of the cumulative compacting of the limestone. Fissuring serves to increase lateral and vertical water transport in the carbonate body of the atoll,[24] possibly resulting in more rapid leakage of fission products. The French authorities claim that no new damage is occurring because the tests are no longer conducted under the reef crown but under the lagoon.[25] This claim is contradicted by underwater observations of the Cousteau mis-

24. Atkinson et al. 1984.
25. Direction des Centres d'Expérimentations Nucléaires 1985.

sion, which discovered recently fallen non-colonized limestone blocks, suggesting that tests were carried out in the months immediately preceding their arrival and that on-going tests are still damaging the reef.[26]

Even the volcanic layer is in danger of being fissured in critical areas by the on-going tests, which means that chambers of vitrified radioactive products may be exposed. Such damage may be more severe than expected because synergistic effects of multiple tests are possible.

Triggering of Landslides, Tsunamis, and Earthquakes

At least one major test-related landslide and consequent tsunami happened in Moruroa, on July 25, 1979. Apparently, the 120-kiloton weapon, which was supposed to be lowered into an 800-meter shaft, got stuck at a depth of 400 meters and could not be dislodged. The French authorities decided to explode the device anyway. This explosion resulted in a major underwater landslide of at least one million cubic meters of coral and rock and created a cavity, probably 140 meters in diameter. The underwater landslide produced a tidal wave comparable to a tsunami, which spread through the Tuamotu Archipelago and injured people on the southern part of Moruroa Atoll.[27]

French authorities initially denied that any mishap had occurred and declared that the tidal wave was of natural origin, but in a publication in 1985 they did acknowledge "the accident of 25 July 1979."[28]

Venting of Gaseous and Volatile Fission Products

Unusual concentrations of short-lived iodine-131 in marine organisms and krypton-85 and tritium in air or water indicate that venting has occurred.

The scientists of the Australia, New Zealand, and Papua New Guinea Mission in 1983 were authorized to carry out a single experiment *in situ* at Moruroa. Their measurements demonstrated a high level of tritium in the interstitial air of the surface terrain. The measured tritium levels were 500 becquerels per liter while the expected con-

26. Cousteau Foundation 1988.
27. Tazieff 1982, Atkinson et al. 1984, and Cousteau Foundation 1988.
28. Direction des Centres d'Expérimentations Nucléaires 1985.

centration due to atmospheric fallout should have been in the range of 0.2 becquerels per liter. The report of this mission offers two explanations for these unexpectedly high tritium levels: either venting of gaseous tritium directly from undergound cavities or a faster groundwater flow rate than admitted.[29]

The venting explanation appears to be the more likely, based on findings of the Cousteau Mission in 1987. Just days after a test, iodine-131 (half-life of 8.05 days) was found in all sediment samples. The same mission measured radioactivity of plankton, which is an even better indicator of venting. In plankton, they found an iodine-131 concentration of 22,000 picocuries per kilogram, by far the strongest radioactivity found during their mission. The Cousteau report stated that iodine-131 most likely reached the surface via the test bore. The report overlooked that fact that the spot with the maximum iodine-131 concentration in sediment was the farthest away from the test site. Nevertheless, because of the short half-life of this radioisotope, its presence could only be attributed to a recent emission. Although authorities at the testing center claimed that this was due to an accidental leak of exceptional character during post-test drilling for purposes of monitoring, the Cousteau Mission was not able to verify that directly.[30] In any case, even such a post-test valve decoupling accident constitutes a venting phenomenon. The fact that the French did not report this venting accident until forced to explain the presence of iodine-131 indicates that venting may be more common than the French nuclear authorities have so far acknowledged.

In summary, two scientific missions, on which major restrictions were imposed, were still able, independently of each other, to find typical indicators of short-term venting.

Medium- and Long-Term Leakage of Fission Products to the Biosphere

According to a model formulated by Hochstein and O'Sullivan (1985), an underground nuclear explosion in rock saturated with seawater can set up an artificial geothermal system. The heat stored in the explosion chamber is on the order of 10^{12} calories per kiloton of yield. In addition, heat generation due to radioactive decay goes on after the explosion of fission bombs, at a rate of about 595 calories per second

29. Atkinson et al. 1984.
30. Cousteau Foundation 1988.

per kiloton of yield. After an explosion, seawater enters the chamber and is heated up by about 25 to 50° Celsius by both stored and newly generated heat. The heated seawater dissolves the glassy materials, liberating the nuclear waste.

At the same time, the heated seawater sets up an artificial geothermal system, which transfers the dissolved nuclear waste slowly upwards through the extended chimney. While the concentration of the radionuclides decreases by diffusion and absorption, the heated cell transferring the radionuclides moves upwards with a speed of about 10 meters per year, according to the computer simulation of Hochstein and O'Sullivan. Under the assumptions of this model, radionuclides from a depth of around 500 meters would reach the cracks of the lagoon in less than 50 years instead of the 500 to 1,000 years assumed by the French authorities.[31]

A first hint that the model of Hochstein and O'Sullivan might be correct was the discovery of cesium-134 by the Cousteau Mission in 1987.[32] In December 1990, too, Greenpeace found cesium-134 in plankton collected outside the 12-mile exclusion zone around Moruroa.[33] While the measured concentrations of cesium-137 are consistent with the consequences of local and global atmospheric tests, the concentrations of cesium-134 are less explicable. Global atmospheric fallout does not contain cesium-134, which is produced by the addition of one neutron to the nucleus of stable cesium-133.

A recent study reviewing the Cousteau Mission's water samples comes to the conclusion that the measured concentrations of cesium-134 are attributable to the underground tests and that only leakage can explain the presence of this radionuclide in Moruroan waters. This study also attempted to identify the source of the leakage by matching the coordinates of French underground tests with the coordinates of the places where samples were taken. Leakage is occurring even faster than initially predicted by the model of Hochstein and O'Sullivan (which assumed equal permeability in all directions), probably only about six years after a test.[34] Venting, which happens occasionally, may open pathways for more rapid leakage than predicted by the model.

The 120 underground tests conducted at Moruroa have in effect turned it into a long-term waste dump. The total amount of plutonium-

31. Hochstein and O'Sullivan 1985.
32. Cousteau Foundation 1988 and Cousteau 1990.
33. Leland 1990.
34. Buske 1990.

239 from these tests and the three at Fangataufa is about 18,450 curies, assuming 150 curies per test. Based on a rough estimate of 2.5 megatons total yield of underground tests, the amount of cesium-137 and strontium-90 dispersed would have been 400,000 curies and 250,000 curies respectively. About three-fourths of the cesium and strontium still remain underground and some may have found its way into the lagoons and ocean. As a repository for nuclear wastes from underground testing, Moruroa is less than ideal. Natural barriers play the most important role in the confinement of nuclear waste.[35] Consequently, a planned storage site should meet very strict criteria including exclusion of water, lack of natural fractures or fissures, and high absorption of radionuclides. According to these criteria, Moruroa is a very poor choice: the geological structure of Moruroa is water-saturated, and there are natural fractures as well as a network of fissures due to the explosions. These fissures affect the volcanic layer. Moreover, the absorption capacity for the basalt of Moruroa as estimated by the French authorities is very low.

In conclusion, Moruroa Atoll is a very poor site for storing nuclear waste of any type. If certain confinement criteria are considered necessary for the storage of waste from nuclear power stations, the same should apply to the storage of waste as a consequence of nuclear explosions. The discovery of cesium-134 indicates only the beginning of long-term leakage from the Moruroa underground "storage" sites.

Transfer of Dissolved Plutonium-239 to the Ocean

Radioactive materials deposited on Moruroa have found their way into the lagoon. The land area of Moruroa has been used to store radioactive waste (including scrap metal, wood, plastic bags, and clothing) in a huge heap on the north coast of the atoll, which covers 30,000 square meters. In addition, on July 21, 1966, a bomb broke apart on the surface of Moruroa, dispersing plutonium-239. This plutonium-239 was confined to the area by fixing it in place with a layer of bitumen. Moruroa was also used as a safety trial area.[36] (A "safety trial" is a test to check whether an atomic bomb will explode on impact with a hard surface—as in the event of a plane crash. In the case of a "safe" bomb, or a "successful" safety trial, the impact does not cause a nuclear detona-

35. Marsily et al. 1977.
36. Confederation Française Democratique du Travail 1981.

tion but breaks apart the bomb, scattering plutonium-239 about the site.) Cyclones hit Moruroa mainly in 1981, washing radioactive waste from the coral rim into the lagoon, including the plutonium-impregnated bitumen.

Due to these waste management practices, the sediment of the lagoon contains an estimated 20 kilograms of plutonium-239. At the time the Australian, New Zealand, and Papua New Guinea Mission visited Moruroa, plutonium-239 concentrations in the air were about four times greater than in continental France. The mission estimated that about 20 gigabecquerels of plutonium-239 from the sediment of the lagoon are transported annually to ocean waters.[37] This is consistent with findings of the Cousteau Mission that concentrations of plutonium-239 in the lagoon entrance are about ten times greater than in the lagoon itself. They also stated that the observed concentrations in the sediment and in the water are much too high to be attributed to global atmospheric fallout and are therefore of local origin and due to remobilization from sedimentary deposits.

There is evidence that plutonium-239 is accumulating in the food chain. While the concentration of plutonium-239 and plutonium-240 are around 0.01 picocuries per liter in the water of the lagoon, the respective concentrations for dry sediment are 1,100 picocuries per kilogram and for dry plankton 9,700 picocuries per kilogram. (Enrichment can be found for cesium-137, also, where the respective concentrations are 0.14 picocuries per liter, 3.5 picocuries per kilogram, and 70 picocuries per kilogram.)[38]

Ciguatera

Ciguatera fish poisoning, discussed in Chapter 5, is a major public health problem in the South Pacific, with nutritional, social, and economic implications. The average annual incidence for the South Pacific area is around 200 cases per 100,000 population per year, but incidences as high as 20,700 per 100,000 population per year are reported for the Gambier Islands.

A review of the epidemiology of ciguatera in French Polynesia from 1960 to 1984 clearly demonstrates a general flare-up in ciguatera, with more than 24,000 cases recorded among a population that grew from

37. Atkinson et al. 1984.
38. Danielsson.

84,500 in 1962 to 174,000 by mid-1985. The incidence rose dramatically through the 1960s, peaking from 1972 to 1975 at 1,200 per 100,000, a 10-fold increase over the 1960 figure.[39] Some of this increase may be due to improved case reporting, but this has never been presented as a major reason for the increase. In the areas most affected, the eastern Tuamotu, Gambier, and Marquesas Archipelagos, the incidence in the 1980s remains at high levels.

The most important cause of ciguatera outbreaks is the disturbance of the sensitive ecology of the coral reef. Natural events, such as storms, earthquakes, and tidal waves, can disturb reef ecology, as can human activities. Nuclear test explosions and the construction of supporting infrastructure have been linked with ciguatera outbreaks.[40]

For example, the Tuamotu Archipelago was more or less free of ciguatera before the early 1960s. Epidemiological studies show that in parallel with the installation and running of the test facilities repeated outbreaks occurred. This is the case for the Hao Atoll (staging base for the testing since 1965, first ciguatera outbreak in 1966), the Gambier Islands (construction of military facilities in 1967, first outbreak in 1968), and Moruroa Atoll (highest density of *Gambierdiscus toxicus* after the Gambier Islands in 1981).[41]

A study by the U.S. Atomic Energy Commission showed no correlation between radioactivity itself and ciguatoxicity in fish.[42] It is most likely that ancillary military activities linked to the nuclear testing facilities, like runway construction, waste dumping, and ship decontamination, are causing ciguatoxicity by disturbance of reef ecology.

39. Bagnis et al. 1985.
40. Ruff 1989a.
41. Inoue 1983.
42. Helfrich 1960.

Chapter 10

CHINA

China has conducted all its nuclear tests at Lop Nor in Sinkiang Province, home to the Uighur people. The location is shown in Figure 11. China exploded its first fission weapon in 1964 and its first thermonuclear weapon in 1967. It conducted 34 tests in all between 1964 and 1988. Of these, 22 were atmospheric tests and the rest underground. China, like France, is not a signatory to the treaty banning atmospheric tests, and it conducted its last one in 1980. In 1986 it announced that it would refrain from further atmospheric testing.

Official data regarding fallout, participation of personnel, dose levels in downwind communities, or environmental contamination have not been released. There do appear to have been problems, possibly from heavy fallout or from accidents, judging from this statement by Qian Xuesen, a senior military official, in 1986:

> Facts are facts. A few deaths have occurred, but generally China has paid great attention to possible accidents. No large disasters have happened.[1]

---

1. Quoted in May 1989, p. 145.

Figure 11

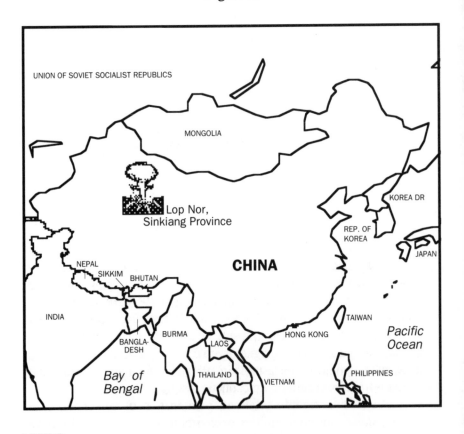

LEGEND

Atmospheric and underground testing

This statement indicates that, at the very least, there have been some deaths attributable to nuclear testing, pointing to the possible occurrence of serious contamination or of accidents. (How the Chinese military defines a "large disaster" is not known.)

At Lop Nor, as in other areas, people have apparently complained of increases in cancer. According to news reports, which may or may not be reliable, there have been demonstrations protesting large increases in cancer incidence. Until the Chinese government releases official data, there is simply no way of telling.

There have been distant hot spots due to Chinese atmospheric testing, according to a Greenpeace compilation of "problems of the nuclear age." Fallout from a September 26, 1976, atmospheric test appears to have settled over the eastern United States. An article in the *New Scientist* reported that at one point, "officials at the Peach Bottom nuclear power plant near Philadelphia feared that their reactor had sprung a leak, so rapidly were their radiation counts rising."[2]

The total amount of plutonium-239 dispersed as a result of 22 Chinese atmospheric tests would be about 3,300 curies, assuming 150 curies per test. The estimate of fission yield of the Chinese tests derived from Table 2, in Chapter 3, is about 12.7 megatons. On this basis, the amount of cesium-137 and strontium-90 dispersed would have been about 2 million curies and 1.3 million curies respectively. Roughly 60 percent of the cesium and strontium still remain in the atmosphere, on the ground, and in bodies of water.

Based on the same assumption about plutonium-239, the total amount of plutonium-239 underground as a result of the 12 Chinese underground tests would be about 1,800 curies. We do not at present have an estimate of the total yield of Chinese underground tests and therefore cannot estimate the fission products remaining underground.

---

2. *New Scientist*, October 14, 1976, as quoted in May 1989, p. 145.

Chapter 11

OTHER COUNTRIES

The only other country known definitely to have conducted a nuclear test is India. India conducted one underground test in the Thar desert in the west in 1974. The test location is shown in Figure 12.

The Indian test is perhaps the best known illustration of the difficulty of distinguishing "peaceful nuclear explosions" from ones with military applications. The Indian government has insisted that the explosion fell into the "peaceful" category and that India has the right to develop nuclear energy for such applications as oil and gas production. Whatever the civilian applications of the test, foreign observers, including those in Pakistan, certainly treated the test as notice of India's capacity to make nuclear weapons.[1]

South Africa is suspected to have conducted a nuclear test as part of a nuclear weapons development program undertaken with possible Israeli collaboration. On September 22, 1979, a U.S. Vela satellite detected a signal in the South Atlantic, southwest of the Cape of Good Hope, that appeared to be from a nuclear explosion. The flash resembled

---

1. Findlay 1990, Chapter 12.

Figure 12

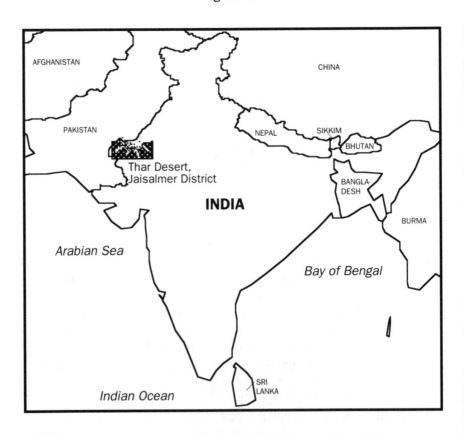

LEGEND

     One underground test

a two-kiloton explosion of a weapon designed to be fired from field artillery.[2] This has not been officially confirmed and is still the subject of considerable controversy.

---

2. Spector 1988, p. 295.

SUMMARY AND CONCLUSIONS

The five nuclear weapons powers have conducted some 1,900 nuclear weapons tests in the atmosphere and underground since the first test, Trinity, was exploded at Alamogordo in the New Mexico desert on July 16, 1945. That amounts to almost one nuclear test per week. In addition, India has conducted one underground test. We regard all nuclear tests as having potential weapons applications. The explosive force of these tests totals about 40,000 times that of the bomb that was dropped on Hiroshima. Figure 13 shows the major test sites worldwide.

Of the total, about 518 nuclear tests were exploded in the atmosphere, underwater, on the surface of the Earth, or in space. These tests (lumped under the rubric "atmospheric" tests) have resulted in pervasive pollution of the Earth, affecting the health of people past, present, and well into the future. Near the test sites, atmospheric tests often resulted in intense fallout and serious harm to local populations and the environment. But they also spread radioactivity all around the globe— radioactivity which persists and will continue to do so for thousands of years. Today, plutonium-239, strontium-90, and cesium-137 constitute pervasive pollutants in our food and water as a result of atmospheric tests.

The grave immediate dangers of atmospheric testing due to fallout led to much public concern and protest and then to the signing of the Limited Test Ban Treaty in 1963 by over 100 countries, including the United States, the Soviet Union, and the United Kingdom. The sig-

159

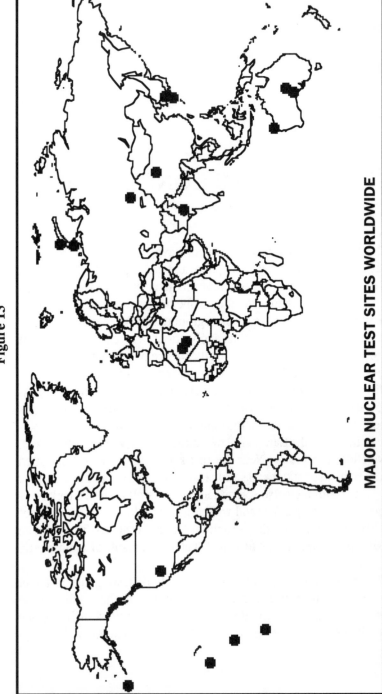

Figure 13

MAJOR NUCLEAR TEST SITES WORLDWIDE

LEGEND
● Major nuclear test site

natories of this treaty agreed to stop atmospheric testing. France and China, however, did not sign and continued atmospheric testing after that—France until 1974 and China until 1980. The United States continues to have a contingency plan to resume atmospheric testing. This may also be true of the other nuclear weapons powers, but in their cases the documentation is not public, preventing us from affirming or negating that hypothesis.

Underground nuclear testing can also result in serious levels of fallout when the explosion is not contained underground but vents into the atmosphere. There is documented evidence of vents from many underground tests.

However, even when the tests are effectively contained and do not result in immediate contamination of the atmosphere, they leave behind a legacy of dangerous long-lived radioactive wastes in an underground environment whose integrity and ability to contain these wastes is literally shattered by the very tests that create the wastes. In the thousands of years that some of the elements will remain radioactive, it seems likely that some radioactive material will escape into groundwater, and thence to the human environment, from at least some of the scores of locations where underground tests have been carried out.

Table 15 summarizes nuclear weapons tests by type, location, and government responsible.

Assessing Health Effects

The effects and risks of nuclear weapons testing have been underestimated. There are three reasons for this:

1. Governments have deliberately withheld information from public view. As data are released from the cover of secrecy, there are clear indications that, in many cases, exposures of people who lived near the test sites or who participated in the testing were more common and the health effects on these populations were greater than previously believed.
2. Studies of the effects of atmospheric tests have been inadequate. Combined with serious deficiencies in the data, this has meant that many of those at high risk have not been properly identified, and their doses may have been considerably underestimated.

Table 15
WORLDWIDE SUMMARY OF NUCLEAR TESTS 1945-1989

Country and location	Atmospheric tests	Underground tests	Total tests	Remarks
U.S.				
Nevada Test Site	100	714	814	
Pacific Areas	106	0	106	includes joint U.S.-U.K. 5 underwater, 6 rocket shots
Hiroshima, Nagasaki	2		2	war-time use
Other	9	11	20	3 space shots
Total U.S.	217	725	942	
Soviet Union				
Kazakhstan	120	347	467	
Novaya Zemlya	90	41	131	
Other	0	115	115	
Total Soviet Union	approx 210	503	713	
Britain				
Australia	12	0	12	
Christmas Island	9	0	9	U.S. tests listed above included in U.S. total
Nevada Test Site	0	(20)	(20)	20 included in U.S. total
Total Britain	21	(20)	(41)	
France				
Algeria	4	10	14	
Polynesia	44	123	167	
Total France	48	133	181	
China, at Lop Nor	22	12	34	not a LTBT signatory
India, Thar desert	0	1	1	not a LTBT signatory
South Africa (with Israel?)	1??	0	1??	
Total, worldwide	518	1,374	1,892	South Africa not included

3. The risks to future generations from underground testing have not yet begun to be studied seriously, in spite of the fact that deposition of long-lived radioactive materials underground without careful construction of barriers to their escape is generally acknowledged to be a highly risky business.

Epidemiologic studies of the health effects and risks of atmospheric testing have been particularly affected by the first two factors. Fallout patterns and doses, both external and internal, to test personnel and local populations were highly variable. Yet, there is very little data on such variability, making it practically impossible to take it into account in assessing risk to specific individuals or in structuring epidemiologic studies so that populations are properly stratified according to risk or dose. As a result of such deficiencies, epidemiologic studies can at once overestimate effects of a given dose of radiation and underestimate the health effects on specific vulnerable groups by failing to identify them accurately.

Atmospheric Testing — Global Effects

Nuclear testing in the atmosphere has resulted in widespread global deposition of radioactive materials. The present inventories of some of the more important ones are:

Strontium-90	11 to 13 million curies
Cesium-137	17 to 21 million curies
Carbon-14	10 million curies
Plutonium-239	255,000 curies

These and other radionuclides created health problems both in local areas and globally. Our estimates of fatal cancers due to the global portion of fallout were derived by applying the latest cancer risk estimates of the Committee on the Biological Effects of Ionizing Radiation of the U.S. National Research Council to dose estimates made by the United Nations Committee on the Effects of Atomic Radiation.

According to our estimates, radioactive materials incorporated into human beings by the end of this century will eventually produce 430,000 cancer fatalities, some of which have already occurred. If we integrate doses out to infinity (in which case the dose from very long-lived carbon-14 dominates), the total number of cancer fatalities grows to 2.4 million. The greatest cancer risk from fallout is in the latitude band between 40 and 50 degrees north, but the greatest number of cancers will occur in the 20 to 30 degrees north band due to the larger number of people residing there.

Atmospheric Testing — Local and Country Effects

Fallout in downwind areas and irradiation of the personnel who participated in nuclear weapons testing has produced many tragedies. For instance, leukemia and other radiogenic cancers have often been found to be associated with participation in the tests, even in epidemiologic studies whose power is seriously compromised by lack of data and by lack of clear identification of personnel at risk.

Fallout caused a tragedy for the people of Rongelap in the Marshall Islands, where the Bravo test conducted by the United States on Bikini in March 1954 resulted in heavy fallout and high levels of radiation, estimated at 190 rems per person on the average. Levels of radiation of about 200 rems are sufficient to increase a person's risk of dying from cancer by about 80 percent. Thyroid disease has been prevalent among this population, especially in children. The Rongelap people remain refugees from their home islands due to fear of residual radiation.

Similar high levels of radiation appear to have resulted in large doses to the population downwind of the Kazakhstan test site in the Soviet Union. While there are problems with the quality of the documentation, and we do not yet have the raw data or peer-reviewed scientific studies of the Soviet situation, the information that has been gathered by various official scientific as well as parliamentary bodies all points to substantial irradiation of large numbers of people. This is corroborated by anecdotal evidence. Our conclusion from examining a considerable amount of difficult and sometimes confusing literature is that at least 1,000 and possibly as many as 40,000 people were heavily irradiated in the downwind area at levels on the order of 200 rems per person. The number may well be considerably greater.

We know of possible heavy fallout from at least one French test in the Pacific in 1967, when two French meteorologists on Tureia were evacuated to a hospital on another island. While the population of Tureia was not evacuated in that year, it was evacuated in its entirety in 1968. The French government still refuses to release data on the test, but insists that radiation doses were low.

There are also indications that there may have been serious irradiation and/or other lethal problems from Chinese testing, since a senior military official has admitted that a "few deaths have occurred." But we have not been able to make any analysis of the matter, as there is practically no public information.

While secrecy with respect to the U.S., British, and Soviet testing programs has diminished greatly in response to public pressure, it is still preventing inquiry into the French and Chinese nuclear weapons tests.

Underground Testing

Venting from many underground tests appears to have been a serious problem in the Soviet Union, as it was in the underground tests in the United States until about 1971. One joint U.S.-British underground test, conducted at the Nevada Test Site, also resulted in some venting.[1] There have been vents from French tests as well. We have no data on Chinese underground tests.

Underground testing has also left large quantities of long-lived radionuclides in scores of locations around the world. Using uniform assumptions about the radionuclides deposited from each test, we have made estimates of the totals for the five nuclear weapons states, which are shown in Table 16. These are estimates of residual radioactivity as of 1989. For strontium and cesium we assume that about one-fourth of the original radioactivity has decayed away. The plutonium-239 is still essentially all there.

These substantial quantities of long-lived radionuclides have been left behind in underground environments seriously fractured by the testing itself, decreasing the ability of that environment to contain the radioactivity. Yet there are no governmental efforts underway to assess the long-term environmental consequences of underground testing.

This lack of effort stands in stark contrast to the efforts of governments to find sites for disposal of radioactive wastes from civilian sources and even from nuclear weapons production. Despite the great efforts that have been made in many countries, such efforts are so controversial that no country has as yet been able to find an acceptable site for disposing of high-level radioactive wastes. On the contrary, most efforts are mired in controversy and public opposition. For instance, the

---

1. U.S. Department of Energy 1989.

Table 16

UNDERGROUND RADIOACTIVITY DUE TO THE TESTING ACTIVITY OF EACH NUCLEAR WEAPONS STATE, AS OF 1989, IN CURIES (ROUNDED TO TWO SIGNIFICANT FIGURES)

Country	Strontium-90	Cesium-137	Plutonium-239	Principal locations
U.S.A.	2,800,000	4,400,000	110,000	Nevada Test Site
U.S.S.R.	2,300,000	3,700,000	75,000	Kazakh Test Site
				Novaya Zemlya
Britain				Nevada, see U.S. total
France	190,000	300,000	18,000	Moruroa, Fangataufa
China	?	?	1,800	Lop Nor
Total	5,300,000	8,400,000	200,000	Totals are rounded, cesium and strontium totals exclude China.

French effort had to be suspended for a period due to fears of the local population about possible contamination of food supplies.

In the United States, after a 25-year process that lurched from one crisis of public confidence to another, the Yucca Mountain site in Nevada was legislatively mandated to be the only site to be investigated. Yet, there are still considerable doubts about the suitability of the site, and its complexity may prevent our even understanding its waste isolation characteristics with confidence. But underground nuclear testing proceeds at nearby Yucca Flats, regardless.

Other local adverse health effects have been caused by activities associated with testing. A major example of such health problems is ciguatera poisoning in the Pacific areas—where France and Britain as well as the United States have tested. Ciguatera poisoning is caused by ingestion of fish contaminated with toxins which are produced in elevated quantities when coral reefs are disrupted by heavy construction and other activities associated with nuclear testing. It causes severe diarrhea and abdominal pain and is accompanied by sensory and/or motor disturbances that can persist for months or years. There is no known cure. Ciguatera poisoning is one of the major health effects common to both atmospheric and underground testing since it is associated with coral reef destruction occasioned by activities related to testing, such as heavy construction and shipping as well as by underground or underwater testing itself. It has severely disrupted fishing and, hence, local food production and commerce.

Concluding Observations

Many aspects of nuclear weapons testing have been characterized by a disregard, sometimes willful, of public health and environment. The willingness shown by nuclear weapons powers to subject people to fallout, and to leave large quantities of radioactive materials underground without any serious study of potential harm to future generations are two broad symptoms of that disregard.

One dramatic example of that disregard, which we explored in Chapter 4, is the way the location of the test site was selected in the United States. We stress here that in this, as in other aspects of the adverse effects of testing, we have not found the U.S. government's behavior to be exceptionally negligent compared to other countries. It is only that we have more information about what the U.S. government has done, due to the greater systematic public pressure and the greater

UNDERGROUND TESTING AREA AT YUCCA FLAT, NEVADA, USA (THE NEVADA TEST SITE). Most underground tests leave craters varying in diameter and depth, depending on yield, depth of burial, and geology.   *Photo: U.S. Department of Energy.*

openness of the political system with respect to the public's right-to-know in the United States.

The Nevada Test Site was chosen during the Korean war, when the U.S. Army and Navy wanted to test nuclear weapons they could use in the field. At the time, there were only large weapons that could be delivered by heavy bombers, which were in the control of the Air Force.

There was a search for sites, which included consideration of radiological aspects. From a radiological safety point of view, it was noted that a site on the East Coast (one south of Cape Hatteras was preferred) would be most suitable, since prevailing westerly winds would blow fallout over the Atlantic. Yet, Nevada was chosen because it was more convenient logistically to Los Alamos, where the weapons to be tested were being fabricated, and because the government already controlled the land.

By selecting a site in the west, the government chose to test in a place it knew would cause fallout over the entire United States due to the prevailing westerly winds. Further, the experience of the very first test was ignored. The Trinity test had resulted in considerable contamination and fallout, including over homes. The recommendation of the radiological safety chief for that test, Colonel Stafford Warren, was that future tests be conducted at a location where there were no inhabited areas within a 150-mile radius. This was ignored in the selection of the Nevada Test Site, with tragic results for many downwind communities. Thus, in evaluating the trade-off between contamination and other factors such as convenience, the latter weighed more heavily in the U.S. government's decision.

In order to make the public accept the possibility of nuclear tests near their homes, U.S. military planners recommended a "reeducation" campaign to "correct" people's "hysterical or alarmist complex" about the dangers of radiation. It was through such reasoning that public education about radiation was replaced by public relations and propaganda. One participant in safety deliberations in 1950 observed, for example, that apparently "the idea of making the public feel at home with neutrons trotting around is the most important angle to get across."[2]

Propaganda and public relations reassurances about safety have dominated the pronouncements of every nuclear weapons state regarding the dangers of fallout and the health and environmental consequen-

---

2. Maj. William R. Sturges, Jr., to Col. Schlatter in a memorandum entitled "Public Relations Conference Concerning Mercury," December 20, 1950, as quoted in Fradkin 1989, p. 97.

ces of testing. And yet they have generally been reluctant to make evidence public for independent scrutiny. We have documented various aspects of such public relations exercises of other nuclear weapons powers. One of them, France, has been so nervous about independent inquiry and protest that it had its agents blow up the ship of an environmental organization, Greenpeace, in Auckland harbor in 1985, killing one person.

While public relations exercises have tended to dominate external relations, there has been a refusal to address serious questions arising from nuclear weapons testing. One of the most egregious aspects of this tradition is that no government has as yet begun a serious effort to estimate the long-term consequences of underground testing.

Health consequences of nuclear weapons testing have fallen most heavily on minority, rural, or disenfranchised populations because governments have tended to situate their test sites in remote areas inhabited by such groups: The United States has tested in areas put under its care for their well-being by the United Nations—the Marshall Islands. Its current test site in Nevada is on land claimed by the Shoshone Indians. The United Kingdom also tested in the Pacific, and in areas of Australia inhabited by aboriginal people. France put its test sites in its colonies—first in Algeria, then in the Pacific. The principal Soviet test site is in Kazakhstan, home to the Kazakhs and far from the Russian homeland. The Novaya Zemlya site similarly belonged to a national minority, the Nenetz people. The Chinese test site at Lop Nor is in an area where most of the people are Uighur, a national minority. Thus, the nuclear weapons powers have tended to visit the worst health and environmental ravages of testing upon rural, minority, and colonized populations by their choice of test sites.

Recommendations

All nuclear weapons testing comes at a real cost to human health and the environment. Thus we reaffirm the long-standing call of IPPNW for an immediate and permanent halt to nuclear weapons testing. Moreover, a number of policy issues are intimately connected with our inquiry into the health and environmental effects of nuclear weapons testing. Our recommendations below arise directly from that inquiry. As such they are more narrowly framed than ones which might arise from a broader consideration of the connections between nuclear testing and the nuclear arms race. But they are nonetheless important in their own right, and we make them here, without prejudice to any positions that might arise out of other, broader considerations relating to testing and nuclear weapons production.

Our first recommendation relates to data and information about weapons testing. All countries that have tested nuclear weapons must make public all information pertaining to the health and environmental effects of their testing programs. This applies with greatest force to France and China, because they remain most secretive. We also recommend universal access to this information, through the United Nations, for example, to permit independent inquiry.

Our second recommendation concerns underground testing. While billions of dollars are being committed throughout the world to study and realize the disposal of highly radioactive wastes, virtually no attention has been paid to the dispersal of long-lasting radionuclides from underground nuclear weapons tests. Until a comprehensive test ban is achieved, we recommend a moratorium on all nuclear weapons testing in order for the long-term environmental effects of weapons testing underground to be studied, understood, and democratically debated.

In addition, we have related recommendations: 1) To avoid conclusions that health risks were small for everyone, epidemiologic studies should identify high-risk populations and assess their exposure and cancer risk, separating them from larger groups for whom the average exposure was smaller. 2) Non-radiologic effects, such as ciguatera poisoning or being displaced from one's home, should be given greater attention when evaluating the health effects of nuclear testing. 3) To recognize and repair the full damage of nuclear weapons testing, special attention should be given to the plight of downwind communities, including colonial, tribal, and national minorities who have so frequently been put in harm's way.

GLOSSARY

Activation product: A material in which radioactivity is induced, by neutron absorption, for example. See **induced radioactivity.**

Alpha radiation: Radiation consisting of a helium ion which is discharged upon radioactive disintegration of certain heavy elements like uranium-238 and radium-226.

Becquerel: A measure of radioactivity of a substance equalling one disintegration per second. One becquerel equals about 27 picocuries.

Beta radiation: Radiation consisting of high-speed electrons or positrons. The term usually refers to electrons, since that is the most common form of beta radiation.

Ciguatera poisoning: Poisoning induced in humans when fish containing ciguatera toxins (or ciguatoxins, for short) are consumed. These toxins are produced by a single-celled organism called *Gambierdiscus toxicus,* which inhabits coral reefs. Outbreaks of poisoning appear to be associated with the disturbance of coral reefs.

Critical mass: The amount of a fissile substance which will result in a self-sustaining chain reaction. This amount depends on the properties of the nucleus and on the geometry into which the material is shaped.

Curie: A measure of radioactivity of a substance equalling 37 billion disintegrations per second, or 2.22 trillion disintegrations per minute. This is the traditional measure of radioactivity and is based on the number of disintegrations per second undergone by one gram of pure radium-226. One curie equals 37 billion becquerels.

Decay-correction: The amount by which the radioactivity of a substance must be reduced after a period of time to account for its radioactive decay during that time.

Dose commitment: The dose imparted by a radionuclide incorporated into the body over a specified period of time, usually 50 years. This concept is used for internal doses because radionuclides, once incorporated into the body, continue to deliver radiation doses until they decay away or are eliminated by biological processes.

Electron: An elementary particle with a negative electrical charge which is much lighter than a proton or a neutron.

Electron-volt: The energy imparted to an electron when it moves through an electric potential difference of one volt. One electron-volt is equal to $1.6 \cdot 10^{-19}$ joules. Abbreviation: eV.

External radiation dose: Radiation dose from sources of radioactivity located outside the body.

Fission: The splitting of the nucleus of an element into fragments. Heavy elements such as uranium release energy when fissioned.

Fission product: An atom created by the fission of heavy elements.

Fusion: The joining of the nuclei of two elements. Fusion of certain light elements such as deuterium and tritium (hydrogen isotopes) gives a net energy release.

Gamma radiation: Electromagnetic radiation of high photon energy (that is, high frequency electromagnetic radiation). The frequencies are far higher than those of the visible range and high enough to cause ionization of elements. Gamma radiation is identical to X-rays of high energy. This is the most penetrating form of radiation.

Gray: A unit of radiation dose equal to 100 rads.

Half-life: The time in which half of a radioactive substance decays away.

Induced radioactivity: Radioactivity produced in certain materials as a result of nuclear reactions, especially by the absorption of neutrons.

Internal radiation dose: Radiation dose to internal organs due to radioactivity inside the body; may consist of any combination of alpha, beta, and gamma radioactivity.

Isotope: A variant of an element with the same number of protons in the nucleus but different numbers of neutrons. Some isotopes of elements may be radioactive, while others may be stable (nonradioactive).

Kilo-electron-volt: One thousand electron-volts. Abbreviation: KeV.

Kiloton: One thousand tons. Used in combination with the concept of TNT equivalent as a measure of yield of nuclear explosives.

Mega-electron-volt: One million electron-volts. Abbreviation: MeV.

Megaton: One million tons. Used in combination with the concept of TNT equivalent as a measure of yield of nuclear explosives.

Milli-: Prefix used with rads, rems, grays, sieverts, and other units to indicate one-thousandth part of the unit.

Micro-: Prefix used with rads, rems, grays, sieverts, and other units to indicate one-millionth part of the unit.

Nano-: Prefix used with rads, rems, grays, sieverts, and other units to indicate one-billionth part of the unit.

Neutron: An elementary particle that is electrically neutral. Neutrons together with protons form the nucleus of an element (except the normal hydrogen nucleus, which consists of a single proton). Neutrons are stable in the nucleus, but unstable in free air, disintegrating into a proton and an electron.

Pico-: Prefix used with rads, rems, grays, sieverts, and other units to indicate one-trillionth part of the unit.

Positrons: An elementary particle with the same mass as an electron but with a positive electrical charge.

Proton: An elementary particle with a positive electrical charge, weighing slightly less than a neutron. Protons and neutrons make up the nuclei of elements.

Rad: A unit of dose equal to the deposition of 100 ergs of energy per gram of material being irradiated.

Radioactivity: The spontaneous release of energy from the nucleus of an atom, in the form of gamma, beta, and/or alpha radiation. Releases of beta and alpha radiation result in the transformation of the atom into a different element (known as transmutation).

Radionuclide: The radioactive isotope of an element.

Rem: A unit of dose that takes into account the relative biological damage due to various kinds of radiation energy absorbed by tissue. In general, the larger the amount of energy deposited per unit length of tissue, the greater the radiation damage per unit of absorbed radiation energy; that is, the greater the ratio of rems to rads. "Linear energy transfer" (LET) is a measure of the relative damage that a unit of radiation energy can do. For gamma radiation, where the energy transfer per unit length is low ("low LET radiation"), rems and rads are essentially equivalent units of radiation dose. For beta radiation, rads and rems are also considered to be equivalent, though the energy transfer per unit length is greater than for gamma radiation. For radiation due to heavy particles—that is, neutrons, protons, and alpha particles—linear energy transfer is high ("high

LET radiation"), and the ratio of rems to rads ranges from two to 40. This ratio is called the "quality factor" of the radiation. The dose in rems is obtained from the dose in rads by multiplying rads by the quality factor. The relationship between the dose in grays (equal to 100 rads) and that in sieverts (equal to 100 rems) is the same as that between rads and rems. A quality factor of 20 is commonly used for alpha radiation and fast neutrons, or when the energy characteristics of the heavy particles are unknown.

Roentgen: A unit measuring gamma radiation dose. It is the quantity of gamma radiation which will produce electrons (in ion pairs) with a total electrical charge of 0.258 millicoulombs in a kilogram of dry air. A roentgen is equal to 0.94 rads. Given the uncertainty about doses that prevails in the circumstances discussed in this study, a roentgen may be taken as essentially equivalent to one rad.

Sievert: A unit of effective dose equal to 100 rems.

Source term: The quantity of a radionuclide emitted into the environment.

Thermonuclear weapon: A nuclear weapon which gets most of its explosive energy from fusion reactions.

TNT equivalent: The unit most commonly used to measure the energy released in nuclear explosions. One ton of TNT is assumed to be equivalent to one billion calories of energy. The energy released by nuclear explosions is generally measured in kilotons and megatons of TNT equivalent.

Yield: The energy released by a nuclear explosion.

REFERENCES

Adams, W.H., et al. 1983. Medical status of Marshallese accidentally exposed to 1954 Bravo fallout radiation, January 1980 through December 1982. Brookhaven National Laboratory.

Allen, Irene, et al. v. the United States of America. Civil case no. C 79-0515-J in U.S. District Court for the District of Utah. Memorandum Opinion, Judge Bruce S. Jenkins, May 9, 1984.

Anspaugh, L.R., Y.E. Ricker, S.C. Black, R.F. Grossman, D.L. Wheeler, B.W. Church, and V.E. Quinn. 1990. Historical exposures of external gamma exposure and collective external gamma exposure from testing at the Nevada Test Site. II. Test series after Hardtack II, 1958, and summary. *Health Physics*, vol. 59, no. 5, pp. 525-532.

Association des Médecins Français pour la Prévention de la Guerre Nucléaire. 1990. Les essais nucléaires français en Polynésie: mission d'études et de rencontres, 9-16 avril 1990. *Médecine et Guerre Nucléaire*, vol. 5, no. 3.

Atkinson, H.R., et al. 1984. Report of a New Zealand, Australian, and Papua New Guinea scientific mission to Moruroa Atoll, October-November 1983. New Zealand Ministry of Foreign Affairs,

Wellington.

Australian Ionising Radiation Advisory Council. 1983. *British Nuclear Tests in Australia—A Review of Operational Safety Measures and of Possible After-Effects* (AIRAC 9).

Australian Radiation Laboratory. 1986. Plutonium-contaminated fragments at the Taranaki site at Maralinga. ARL/TRO75.

Australian Radiation Laboratory. 1988. Tietkens Plain Karst--Maralinga. ARL/TRO81.

Australian Radiation Laboratory. 1989. Plutonium contamination in the Maralinga Tjarutja lands. ARL/TRO85.

Australian Radiation Laboratory. 1990. Inhalation hazard assessment at Maralinga and Emu. ARL/TRO87.

Bagnis, R. 1969. Naissance et développement d'une flambée de ciguatera dans un atoll des Tuamotu. *Révue des Corps de Santé*, vol. 10, no. 6.

Bagnis, R. 1981. Etude morphologique, biologique, toxicologique et écologique de l'agent causal princeps de la ciguatera, le péridinien *Gambierdiscus toxicus*. Thésis, Université de Bordeaux, II.

Bagnis, R. 1982. La ciguatera dans les atolls des Tuamotu. SPC/Atolls/WP, 12, 22 March. Noumea: South Pacific Commission.

Bagnis, R., et al. 1985. Epidemiology of ciguatera in French Polynesia from 1960 to 1984. In *Proceedings of the Fifth International Coral Reef Congress, Tahiti, Vol. 4*, ed. by C. Gabrie and B. Salvat. Moorea: Antenne Museum-ephe.

Balmukhanov, S. 1990. Lecture at conference of European affiliates of the International Physicians for the Prevention of Nuclear War, Coventry, U.K., September.

Banner, A.M. 1974. The biological origin and transmission of ciguatera. In *Bioactive Compounds from the Sea*, ed. by H.J. Humm and

C.E. Lane. New York: Marcel Dekker.

Bartsch, A., and E.F. McFarren. 1962. Fish poisoning: a problem in food intoxication. *Pacific Science,* vol. 16, no. 1.

Blakeway, D., and S. Lloyd-Roberts. 1985. *Fields of Thunder: Testing Britain's Bomb.* London: Unwin.

Boag, J.W., J. Fielding, J.H. Humphrey, A. Jacobs, P. Lindop, J. Rotblat, and J.A. Thompson. 1983. Letter. *Lancet,* vol. 1, p. 815, April 9.

Bramlitt, E.T. 1988. Plutonium mining for cleanup. *Health Physics,* vol. 55.

British Broadcasting Corporation. 1983. *Clouds Over Christmas Island.* BBC Panorama television program, ed. by George Carey, prod. by Denys Blakeway.

Broad, William J. 1990. A mountain of trouble. *The New York Times Magazine,* Nov. 18.

Burrows, A.S., R.S. Norris, W.M. Arkin, and T.B. Cochran. 1989. *French Nuclear Testing 1960-1988.* Natural Resources Defense Council, Washington, D.C.

Buske, N. 1990. Cesium 134 at Moruroa—review of the Calypso water samples. SEARCH Technical Services, Davenport.

Butement, W.A.S., L.J. Dwyer, C.E. Eddy, L.H. Martin, and E.W. Titterton. 1957. Radioactive fallout in Australia from Operation "Mosaic." *Australian Journal of Science,* vol. 20, pp. 125-135.

Butrico, Frank. Subject: Discussion with Representative Stringfellow in St. George, Utah. Memorandum to William S. Johnson, Off-Site Operations Officer, N.P.G., May 28, 1953.

Carter, Melvin W., and A. Alan Moghissi. 1977. Three decades of nuclear testing. *Health Physics,* vol. 33, July.

Church, B.W., D.L. Wheeler, C.M. Campbell, R.V. Nutley, and L.R. Anspaugh. 1990. Overview of the Department of Energy's Off-site

Radiation Exposure Review Project (ORERP). *Health Physics*, vol. 59, no. 5, pp. 503-510.

Cochran, T.B., W.M. Arkin, R.S. Norris, and J.I. Sands. 1989. *Soviet Nuclear Weapons.* (Nuclear Weapons Databook, vol. 4.) New York: Harper and Row.

Commission of People's Deputies. 1990. Report to the Supreme Soviet's Subcommittee on Power Engineering and Nuclear Ecology of the Committee on Ecology and Rational Use of Natural Resources, February 8. Translation by the Soviet Committee of Physicians for the Prevention of Nuclear War.

Conard, R.A. 1984. Late radiation effects in Marshall Islanders exposed to fallout 28 years ago. In *Radiation Carcinogenesis Epidemiology and Biological Significance,* ed. by J.D. Boice, Jr. and J.F. Fraumeni, Jr. New York: Raven Press.

Conard, R.A., et al. 1980. Review of medical findings in a Marshallese population twenty-six years after accidental exposure to radioactive fallout. Brookhaven National Laboratory.

Confédération Française Démocratique du Travail. 1981. Contamination de Moruroa. Statement by CFDT, Section BIII, Paris.

Connor, S. 1988. Risk and the radioactive service. *New Scientist,* vol. 117, February 4, pp. 30-31.

Connor, S., and A. Thomas. 1985. Minister withheld data on A-tests. *New Scientist,* vol. 106, April 18.

Cooney, James P. (Colonel and Radiological Safety Officer). Memorandum to Rear Admiral Parsons, May 11, 1948. Annex "B" in U.S. Commanding Lieutenant General J.E. Hull's memorandum to the U.S. Army Chief of Staff, "Subject: location of proving ground for atomic weapons."

Cousteau, J. 1990. Assessment of artificial radionuclides issued from French nuclear bomb testing at Moruroa (French Polynesia). *Environmental Technology,* vol. 11.

Cousteau Foundation. 1988. Scientific Mission of the Calypso at the Moruroa Nuclear Test Site. Paris. (Official translation by External Assessments Bureau, Ministry of External Relations and Trade, Wellington.)

Danielsson, B. 1984. Under the cloud of secrecy: the French nuclear tests in the south-eastern Pacific. *Ambio*, vol. 13, no. 5-6.

Danielsson, B., and M.T. Danielsson. 1986. *Poisoned Reign: French Nuclear Colonialism in the Pacific*. Melbourne: Penguin Books.

Danielsson, M.T., and B. Danielsson. 1985. The Mangareva story: Greenpeace vs. *Gambierdiscus. Pacific Islands Monthly*, vol. 56, no. 12.

Darby, S.C., and R. Doll. Letter. *British Medical Journal*, vol. 296, pp. 716-717.

Darby, S.C., et al. 1988a. Mortality and cancer incidence in U.K. participants in U.K. atmospheric nuclear weapons tests and experimental programmes. National Radiological Protection Board, Oxon.

Darby, S.C., G.M. Kendall, T.P. Fell, J.A. O'Hagan, C.R. Muirhead, J.R. Ennis, A.M. Ball, J.A. Dennis, and R. Doll. 1988b. A summary of the mortality and incidence of cancer in men from the United Kingdom who participated in the United Kingdom's atmospheric tests and experimental programmes. *British Medical Journal*, vol. 296, pp. 332-338.

Dean, Gordon (Chairman, U.S. Atomic Energy Commission). 1950a. Memorandum to Honorable Robert LeBaron, Chairman, Military Liaison Committee to the Atomic Energy Commission, July 13, 1950. Coordinating Information Center Library, no. 101168.

Dean, Gordon (Chairman, U.S. Atomic Energy Commission). 1950b. Location of proving ground for atomic weapons—selection of a continental atomic test site. Report by the Director of Military Application. U.S. AEC Document 141/7, December 13.

Defense Nuclear Agency. 1982. Fact sheet. Subject: nuclear test personnel review. Washington, D.C.

Direction des Centres d'Expérimentations Nucléaires. 1985. Dossier
no. 1: Organization et fonctionnement des Centres d'Expérimentations Nucléaires. Paris.

Dwyer, L.J., J.H. Martin, D.J. Stevens, and E.W. Titterton. 1959.
Radioactive fallout in Australia from Operation Antler. *Australian
Journal of Science*, vol. 22, pp. 97-106.

Eisenbud, Merril. 1987. *Environmental Radioactivity*. San Diego:
Academic Press.

Eisenbud, M. 1989. Letter from M. Eisenbud to Henry Kohn, Decem-
ber 13, 1987, cited in H. Kohn, *Rongelap Reassessment Project
Report,* corrected edition, p. 54. Rongelap Reassessment Project,
Berkeley.

Findlay, Trevor. 1990. *Nuclear Dynamite: The Peaceful Nuclear
Explosions Fiasco*. Brassey's Australia.

Firth, S. 1987. *Nuclear Playground*. Sydney: Allen and Unwin.

Fradkin, Philip L. 1989. *Fallout: An American Tragedy*. Tucson:
University of Arizona Press.

Franke, Bernd. 1989a. Is Rongelap Atoll safe? Institute for Energy and
Environmental Research, Takoma Park, Maryland.

Franke, Bernd. 1989b. Statement before the Subcommittee on Insular
and International Affairs of the House Interior and Insular Affairs
Committee, House of Representatives, U.S. Congress,
November 16.

Franke, Bernd. 1990. Why the Rongelap Reassessment Project did not
fulfill its mission: a report to the Rongelap Atoll Local Government.
Institute for Energy and Environmental Research, Takoma Park,
Maryland.

French Atomic Energy Commission. Memorandum of the Directorate
for Nuclear Test Centers, August 25, 1988. Villecoublay, France.

Gardner, M. 1988. Cancer among participants in tests of British nuclear weapons. Editorial. *British Medical Journal,* vol. 296, pp. 309-310.

Gardner, M. 1990. Cancer among participants in British atmospheric nuclear weapons tests in the Pacific. *British Medical Journal,* vol. 300.

Glasstone, Samuel, and Philip Dolan. 1977. *The Effects of Nuclear Weapons.* Washington, D.C.: Department of the Army.

Greenpeace. 1990. Fact sheet on nuclear tests.

Greenpeace New Zealand. 1985. *French Polynesia: The Nuclear Tests—a Chronology.* Auckland, New Zealand.

Hadlington, S. 1988. Cancer risk slightly higher for U.K. nuclear test participants. *Nature,* vol. 383, February 4.

Hamer, M. 1988. Maralinga exposure. *New Scientist,* vol. 117, January 7.

Helfrich, P. 1960. A study of the possible relationship between radioactivity and toxicity in fishes from the Central Pacific. U.S. Atomic Energy Commission, Technical Information Service Publication No. TID-5748, Oak Ridge, Tennessee.

Hochstein, M.P., and M.J. O'Sullivan. 1985. Geothermal systems created by underground nuclear testing. In *Proceedings of the 7th New Zealand Geothermal Workshop.*

Holzman, B.G. (U.S. Air Force Colonel). Subject: site for atomic bomb experiments. Memorandum to Admiral Parsons, April 21, 1948. Annex "A" in U.S. Commanding Lieutenant General J.E. Hull's memorandum to the U.S. Army Chief of Staff, "Subject: location of proving ground for atomic weapons."

House Veterans Affairs Committee. Record of hearing, May 24, 1983. U.S. House of Representatives, Washington, D.C.

Hughes, S. European Parliament session, December 1, 1988. Document A2-0283/88.

Hull, J.E. (U.S. Commanding Lieutenant General). No date. Subject: location of proving ground for atomic weapons. Memorandum to the U.S. Army Chief of Staff.

Hutchinson, H.B. (U.S. Navy Captain). Subject: progress report—Project Nutmeg. Memorandum for Admiral Parsons. U.S. DOE Archives 326 Atomic Energy Commission, Collection DMA Files, Box 3865, November 10, 1948.

Inoue, A. 1983. Distribution of a toxic dinoflagellate *Gambierdiscus toxicus,* in French Polynesia. Memoirs of the Kagoshima University Research Center for the South Pacific, vol. 4, no. 1, pp. 9-18.

Knox, E.G., T. Sorahan, and A. Stewart. 1983. Cancer following nuclear weapons tests. *Lancet,* vol. 1, p. 815, April 9.

Kotrady, Konrad P. 1977. The Brookhaven Medical Program to Detect Radiation Effects in Marshallese People: a comparison of the people's attitudes vs. the program's attitudes.

Lapp, Ralph E. 1958. *Voyage of the Lucky Dragon.* New York: Harper and Brothers.

Leland, B. 1990. Greenpeace finds trace radioactivity near Moruroa. *PeaceNet,* Dec. 10.

Lessard, E.T., R. Miltenberger, R. Conard, S. Musolino, J. Naidu, A. Moorthy, and C. Schopfer. 1985. Thyroid absorbed dose for people at Rongelap, Utirik, and Sifo on March 1, 1954. BNL 51882. Brookhaven National Laboratory, Upton, New York.

Lewis, N.D. 1984. Ciguatera in the Pacific: incidence and implications for marine resource development. In *Seafood Toxins,* ed. by E.P. Ragelis. American Chemical Society Symposium Series 262, Washington, D.C.

Lewis, N.D. 1984. Ciguatera: parameters of a tropical health problem. *Human Ecology,* vol. 12.

List, Robert J. 1954. The transport of atomic debris from Operation Upshot-Knothole. NYO-4602, June 25. U.S. Atomic Energy Commission, Washington, D.C.

Makhijani, Arjun, and David Albright. 1983. The irradiation of personnel during Operation Crossroads. International Radiation Research and Training Institute, Washington, D.C.

Makhijani, Arjun, and John Kelly. 1985. Target: Japan—the decision to bomb Hiroshima and Nagasaki. Published in Japanese under the title *Why Japan?* Tokyo: Kyoikusha.

Makhijani, Arjun. 1989. Reducing the risks. Institute for Energy and Environmental Research, Takoma Park, Maryland.

Marsily, G., E. Lepoux, A. Barbreau, and J. Margat. 1977. Nuclear waste disposal: can the geologist guarantee isolation? *Science.*

Marston, H.R. 1958. The accumulation of radioactive iodine in the thyroids of grazing animals subsequent to atomic weapons tests. *Australian Journal of Biological Sciences,* vol. 11, pp. 382-398.

May, John. 1989. *The Greenpeace Book of the Nuclear Age.* Pantheon Books.

McEwan, A.C. 1988. Cancers in J-Force and Christmas Island veterans. *Radiation Protection News and Notes* (National Radiation Laboratory, Christchurch, New Zealand), vol. 1.

McEwan, A.C. 1990. Is it radiation: New Zealand navy test veterans. *Radiation Protection News and Notes* (National Radiation Laboratory, Christchurch, New Zealand), vol. 11.

Medico-Legal Board of Operation Crossroads. Minutes of the August 10, 1946 meeting.

Milliken, R. 1986. *No Conceivable Injury.* Penguin Books Australia.

National Research Council. 1980. *The Effects on Populations of Exposure to Low Levels of Ionizing Radiation* (BEIR III). Washington, D.C.: National Academy Press.

National Research Council. 1988. *Health Risks of Radon and Other In-*

ternally Deposited Alpha Particle Emitters (BEIR IV). Washington, D.C.: National Academy Press.

National Research Council. 1990. *Health Effects of Exposure to Low Levels of Ionizing Radiation* (BEIR V). Washington, D.C.: National Academy Press.

Natural Resources Defense Council. 1988. Known U.S. nuclear weapons tests, July 1945 to 31 December 1987.

O'Keefe, Bernard J. 1983. *Nuclear Hostages.* Boston: Houghton Mifflin Company.

Parsons, Rear Admiral. Subject: site for atomic bomb experiments, May 12, 1948. Appendix to U.S. Commanding Lieutenant General J.E. Hull's memorandum to the U.S. Army Chief of Staff, "Subject: location of proving ground for atomic weapons."

Pearce, N., et al. 1990. Mortality and cancer incidence in New Zealand participants in United Kingdom nuclear weapons tests in the Pacific. Wellington School of Medicine.

Pearce, N. 1990. Follow-up of New Zealand participants in British atmospheric nuclear weapons tests in the Pacific. *British Medical Journal,* vol. 300.

Randall, J.E. 1980. A survey of ciguatera at Enewetak and Bikini, Marshall Islands, with notes on the systematics and food habits of ciguatoxic fishes. *Fishery Bulletin,* vol. 78, no. 2, pp. 201-249.

Reines, Frederick, note-taker. 1950. Discussion of radiological hazards associated with a continental test site for atomic bombs, August 1. LAMS-1173. Los Alamos Scientific Laboratory, University of California, Livermore, California.

Robinson, D. 1985. *Just Testing.* London: Collins Harvill.

Robison, W.L., et al. 1977. *Dose Assessment at Bikini Atoll.* UCRL-51879. Lawrence Livermore National Laboratory, Livermore, California.

Robison, W.L., and W.A. Phillips. 1989. Estimates of the radiological dose from ingestion of 137Cs and 90Sr to infants, children, and adults in the Marshall Islands. UCRL-53917. Lawrence Livermore National Laboratory, Livermore, California.

Robotham, Rob. 1984. British A-bomb tests in Australia: a blast from the past. *Peace Studies* (Victorian Association of Peace Studies, Fitzroy), no. 1 (March).

Roser, M.E. Subject: ACTION: Marshall Islands Programs. Memorandum to the Secretary and Deputy Secretary, Department of Energy, March 16, 1982.

Royal Commission. 1985. *The Report of the Royal Commission into British Nuclear Tests in Australia,* vol. 1, vol. 2, and Conclusions and Recommendations. Australian Government Publishing Service.

Ruff, T.A. 1989a. Ciguatera in the Pacific: a link with military activities. *Lancet,* vol. 1, no. 8631, pp. 201-205.

Ruff, T.A. 1989b. Fish poisoning in the Pacific: the military connection. Working Paper No. 63, Peace Research Centre, Research School of Pacific Studies, Australian National University, Canberra.

Ruff, T.A. 1990. Bomb tests attack the food chain. *Bulletin of the Atomic Scientists,* vol. 46, no. 2, pp. 32-34.

Schleien, Bernard. 1981. External radiation exposure to the offsite population from nuclear tests at the Nevada Test Site between 1951 and 1970. *Health Physics,* vol. 41.

Shapiro, Jacob. 1990. *Radiation Protection,* third edition. Cambridge, Mass., and London: Harvard University Press.

Smith, J. 1985. *Clouds of Deceit.* London: Faber and Faber.

Smith, W., ed. 1989. Underground nuclear explosions in the Tuamotu Archipelago. Geophysics Dept, DSIR, Wellington.

Sorahan, T. 1988. Letter. *British Medical Journal,* vol. 296, p. 716.

South Australian Health Commission. 1981. A survey of disease that may be related to radiation among Pitjantjatjara on remote reserves.

South Australian Health Commission. 1983-1984. The feasibility of demonstrating long-term somatic and heritable health effects of ionizing radiation on local Aboriginal populations.

South Pacific Commission. 1988. Ciguatera fish poisoning. SPC/Fisheries 20/Information Paper 16, July 29. Noumea: South Pacific Commission.

South Pacific Epidemiological and Health Information Service. 1974-1990. *Annual Reports, 1973-89*. Noumea: South Pacific Commission.

Spector, Leonard S. 1988. *The Undeclared Bomb*. Cambridge, Massachusetts: Ballinger.

Stevens, Walter, D.C. Thomas, J.L. Lyon, J.E. Till, R.A. Kerber, S.L. Simon, R.D. Lloyd, and N.A. Elghany. 1990. Leukemia in Utah and radioactive fallout from the Nevada Test Site. *Journal of the American Medical Association*, vol. 264, no. 5, pp. 585-591.

Swedish National Defense Research Institute. 1987. Computer printout of nuclear explosions. Hagsfors Observatory.

Tame, A., and P.J. Robotham. 1982. *Maralinga British A-Bomb Australian Legacy*. Melbourne: Fontana/Collins.

Tamplin, A.R. 1966. Prediction of radionuclide burdens in man. In *Program Book for the Advisory Committee for Biology and Medicine of the United States Atomic Energy Commission, Part II*. UCRL-14739. Lawrence Livermore Radiation Laboratory, University of California, Livermore, California.

Tazieff, H. 1982. Rapport d'Haroun Tazieff sur l'ensemble de la Mission Scientifique en Polynésie Française. Paris.

Technical Assessment Group, Department of Primary Industries and Energy. 1990. *Rehabilitation of Former Nuclear Test Sites in Australia*. Canberra: Australian Government Publishing Service.

Tokhtarov, Tanibergen. 1990. The situation in the neighborhood of the Semipalatinsk nuclear test site. Report submitted to the Supreme Soviet of Kazakh SSR. Translated by the Soviet Committee of Physicians for the Prevention of Nuclear War and Alexander Shlyakhter, Harvard University.

Tsyb Commission. 1989. Report. Translated by the Soviet Committee of Physicians for the Prevention of Nuclear War.

United Kingdom Air Ministry. 1957. *The Nuclear Handbook for Instructors and Staff Officers.*

United Nations Scientific Committee on the Effects of Atomic Radiation (UNSCEAR). 1982. *Ionizing Radiation: Sources and Biological Effects.* Report to the General Assembly, with annexes. New York: United Nations.

United Nations Scientific Committee on the Effects of Atomic Radiation (UNSCEAR). 1988. *Sources, Effects and Risks of Ionizing Radiation.* Report to the General Assembly, with annexes. New York: United Nations.

U.S. Atomic Energy Commission. 1954. Radioactive debris from Operations Upshot and Knothole. NYO-4552, June 25. Washington, D.C.

U.S. Atomic Energy Commission. 1955. Atomic test effects in the Nevada Test Site region.

U.S. Atomic Energy Commission. 1956. Transcript of the 54th meeting of the Advisory Committee on Biology and Medicine (ACBM), January 13-14, New York, New York. In Coordinating Information Center Library (CIC), Las Vegas, Nevada.

U.S. Atomic Energy Commission. 1961. Minutes of the 88th meeting of the Advisory Committee on Biology and Medicine (ACBM), September 8-9.

U.S. Atomic Energy Commission and U.S. Department of Defense. Memorandum of understanding, February 11, 1969. In Coordinating Information Center Library (CIC), Las Vegas, Nevada.

U.S. Atomic Energy Commission. 1974. Policy Session Item, SECY-75-542, April 16. In U.S. Department of Energy Archives, Germantown, Maryland.

U.S. Congress. HR2372, with revisions incorporated from HR4739, Section 3139 and 3140.

U.S. Congress, Office of Technology Assessment. 1989. *The Containment of Underground Nuclear Explosions.* OTA-1 SC-41 4. Washington, D.C.

U.S. Congress, Office of Technology Assessment. 1991. *Complex Cleanup: the Environmental Legacy of Nuclear Weapons Production.* OTA-O-484. Washington, D.C.

U.S. Department of Energy. 1982a. *The Meaning of Radiation for those Atolls in the Northern Part of the Marshall Islands that were Surveyed in 1978.* A bilingual report in Marshallese and English. Washington, D.C.

U.S. Department of Energy. 1982b. Eniwetak Radiological Support Project, final report. NVO-213.

U.S. Department of Energy. 1989. Announced United States nuclear tests, July 1945 through December 1988. NVO-209, September.

U.S. Environmental Protection Agency, Office of Radiation Programs. 1986. Interim recommendations on doses to persons exposed to transuranium elements in the general environment. Washington, D.C.

U.S. Federal Radiation Council. 1960. Radiation protection guidance for federal agencies. *Federal Register,* May 18.

U.S. General Accounting Office. 1987. Radiation exposures for some cloud-sampling personnel need to be reexamined. GAO/RCED-87-134.

Warren, Stafford L. Subject: Report on Test II at Trinity, 16 July 1945. Memorandum to Major General Groves, July 21, 1945. National Archives, Manhattan Project Papers.

Warren, Stafford L. Memorandum to Commander Task Group 1.3, USS Haven, August 13, 1946.

Zheutlin, Peter. 1990. Kazakhstan: life and death in the shadow of the mushroom cloud. *Los Angeles Times,* April 1.